THE ALTERNATIVE

A Play for Ireland

by Michael Patrick and Oisín Kearney

‖SAMUEL FRENCH‖

samuelfrench.co.uk

For Amateur Production Enquiries

United Kingdom and World
EXCLUDING NORTH AMERICA
plays@samuelfrench.co.uk
020 7255 4302/01

Each title is subject to availability from Samuel French, depending upon country of performance.

The script may differ to what is presented on stage.

THINKING ABOUT PERFORMING A SHOW?

There are thousands of plays and musicals available to perform from Samuel French right now, and applying for a licence is easier and more affordable than you might think

From classic plays to brand new musicals, from monologues to epic dramas, there are shows for everyone.

Plays and musicals are protected by copyright law, so if you want to perform them, the first thing you'll need is a licence. This simple process helps support the playwright by ensuring they get paid for their work and means that you'll have the documents you need to stage the show in public.

Not all our shows are available to perform all the time, so it's important to check and apply for a licence before you start rehearsals or commit to doing the show.

LEARN MORE & FIND THOUSANDS OF SHOWS

Browse our full range of plays and musicals, and find out more about how to license a show

www.samuelfrench.co.uk/perform

Talk to the friendly experts in our Licensing team for advice on choosing a show and help with licensing

plays@samuelfrench.co.uk   020 7387 9373

Acting Editions

BORN TO PERFORM

Playscripts designed from the ground up to work the way you do in rehearsal, performance and study

---

Larger, clearer text for easier reading

Wider margins for notes

Performance features such as character and props lists, sound and lighting cues, and more

---

+ CHOOSE A SIZE AND STYLE TO SUIT YOU

  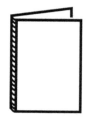

STANDARD EDITION	SPIRAL-BOUND EDITION	LARGE EDITION
Our regular paperback book at our regular size	The same size as the Standard Edition, but with a sturdy, easy-to-fold, easy-to-hold spiral-bound spine	A4 size and spiral bound, with larger text and a blank page for notes opposite every page of text – perfect for technical and directing use

LEARN MORE | **samuelfrench.co.uk/actingeditions**

Other plays by MICHAEL PATRICK AND OISÍN KEARNEY
published by Samuel French

My Left Nut

FIND PERFECT PLAYS TO PERFORM AT
www.samuelfrench.co.uk/perform

ABOUT THE AUTHORS

MICHAEL PATRICK

Michael was born and raised in Belfast, where he still lives today. He originally studied Physics at the University of Cambridge, before training as an actor at Mountview Academy of Theatre Arts. He still feels like a bit of a fraud when he calls himself a 'writer'. But he recently changed his twitter bio to read Actor / Writer. So that's progress.

OISÍN KEARNEY

Oisín is from Warrenpoint, Co. Down. He studied Politics at the University of Cambridge. He now lives in Belfast, where he works as a writer and director for stage and screen.

The pair met at Churchill College Cambridge, together they ran the University Ireland Society and created theatre. For the past number of years they've made theatre in Belfast with their company Pan Narrans Theatre; Michael acting and Oisín directing.

The Alternative is the second stage play they've written together.

CO-AUTHOR'S NOTE

When we applied to Fishamble's 'A Play for Ireland' scheme, the brief was to submit a single A4 page for a script idea. We thought we may as well send in something mad. We never thought we would get through the first round, never mind get selected as the final play.

We cannot thank Fishamble enough for believing in us. This play is so much bigger than our last one – in every sense of the word. It's never something we would have envisaged writing without the support of Fishamble backing us. They gave us the drive and the confidence to go a little bit crazy.

As Irish citizens living in Northern Ireland we've always had an interest in identity and what it means to be Irish. The ideas in this play have always existed in our heads, this is our attempt to try and corral them onto a page. 2021 marks 100 years since the partition of Ireland. The future of the relationship between Ireland and the United Kingdom is as uncertain as ever. In order to move forward we need to envisage many alternatives, and open our eyes to every possibility.

And it's always fun to try to offend as many people as we can.

MUSIC USE NOTE

Licensees are solely responsible for obtaining formal written permission from copyright owners to use copyrighted music in the performance of this play and are strongly cautioned to do so. If no such permission is obtained by the licensee, then the licensee must use only original music that the licensee owns and controls. Licensees are solely responsible and liable for all music clearances and shall indemnify the copyright owners of the play(s) and their licensing agent, Samuel French, against any costs, expenses, losses and liabilities arising from the use of music by licensees. Please contact the appropriate music licensing authority in your territory for the rights to any incidental music.

USE OF COPYRIGHT MUSIC

A licence issued by Samuel French Ltd to perform this play does not include permission to use the incidental music specified in this copy.

Where the place of performance is already licensed by the PERFORMING RIGHT SOCIETY (PRS) a return of the music used must be made to them. If the place of performance is not so licensed then application should be made to the PRS, 2 Pancras Square, London, N1C 4AG.

A separate and additional licence from
PHONOGRAPHIC PERFORMANCE LTD,
1 Upper James Street, London W1F 9DE (www.ppluk.com)
is needed whenever commercial recordings are used.

IMPORTANT BILLING AND CREDIT REQUIREMENTS

If you have obtained performance rights to this title, please refer to your licensing agreement for important billing and credit requirements.

FIRST PRODUCTION

The Alternative was first previewed at The Everyman, Cork, before opening at the Pavilion Theatre, Dún Laoghaire, as part of the Dublin Theatre Festival, on 26 September 2019.

Cast

URSULA LYSAGHT	Karen Ardiff
RICHARD DEVLIN	Lorcan Cranitch
GRAINNE DEVLIN	Maeve Fitzgerald
PATRICK	Fionntán Larney
JOHN FITZGIBBON	Rory Nolan
HANNAH MURRAY	Rachel O'Byrne
PETER KEOGH	Arthur Riordan

Cast (on screen)

NIAMH	Bríd Ní Neachtain
REPORTER	Peter Daly
VOX POPS	Fionn Foley
	Patrick Martins
	Mary Murray
	Roseanna Purcell
	Gene Rooney

Cast (voiceovers)

Helen Norton
Nick Dunning

Production Team

Director Jim Culleton
Set Designer Maree Kearns
Lighting Designer Mark Galione
Sound Designer Denis Clohessy
Costume Designer Saileóg O'Halloran
Video Designer Oisín Kearney
Hair and Makeup Val Sherlock
Production Managers Marie Tierney & Sarah Keane
Stage Manager Fiona Keller
Assistant Stage Managers Sarah Purcell & Sean Walsh

Fight Director Bryan Burroughs
Vision Mixer Sean Walsh
Dramaturg Gavin Kostick
Choral Director Ruaidhrí Ó Dálaigh
Irish Translation by Fionn Foley & Siobhán Ní Chiobháin
Assistant Director* Martha Fitzgerald
Assistant Designer* KathyAnn Murphy
Production Coordinator Ronan Carey
Marketing Chandrika Narayanan-Mohan
Marketing Intern Niamh Ní Fhlatharta
PR O'Doherty Communications
Graphic Design Publicis Dublin
Producer Eva Scanlan

AV Director, Camera Oisín Kearney
AV Producer Ciara Elizabeth Smyth
Camera & Graphics Pete Graham
Camera Federico Rea
Campaign Poster Designer Naomi Sheehan
AV Graphic Designer Chris Scott

*Training placements as part of Fishamble's company-in-association status at UCD.

The production runs for approximately two hours, including an interval.

The Alternative was chosen for production at the end of *A Play for Ireland*, a two-year artist development initiative in 2018/19, to mark Fishamble's 30th year.

BIOGRAPHIES

Michael Patrick (actor & writer from Belfast) and **Oisín Kearney** (director & writer from Warrenpoint) work as a writing pair. In 2017 they co-wrote the award-winning *My Left Nut*, which was developed through the Show in a Bag programme run by Fishamble, ITI and Dublin Fringe. It was nominated for the best show under one hour at the Dublin Fringe awards and won a Summerhall Lustrum Award at the Edinburgh Fringe. Michael and Oisín have since adapted *My Left Nut* into a three-part series for BBC Three. They are also a part of the BBC Belfast Voices screenwriting scheme and have written for BBC NI's *Soft Border Patrol*.

Oisín has localised Willy Russell's scripts of *Educating Rita* and *Shirley Valentine* to 1980s Belfast for The Lyric Theatre. He is currently resident Assistant Director for the Lyric Theatre and previously has assisted on *Educating Rita* and *Good Vibrations*. On the latter, he worked closely with Colin Carberry and Glenn Patterson on their translation of the story from screen to stage. Theatre directing credits include *My Left Nut, How These Desperate Men Talk* and *I, Banquo*. Documentary directing credits include *All For Show* (BBC NI True North), *Bbeyond* (BBC Arts Show), *Borderlands* and *Unfinished Revolution* (De Correspondent, NPO2), and *BOJAYÁ: Caught In The Crossfire* (Hot Docs Film Festival 2019).

As an actor, Michael has worked with The Abbey Theatre, The Lyric Theatre, Tinderbox, NI Opera and has appeared on *Game of Thrones, Death and Nightingales, Krypton, Soft Border Patrol* and *My Left Nut*. At time of publishing he is acting in the Royal Shakespeare Company's 2019/20 season.

Jim Culleton is the artistic director of Fishamble, for which he has directed productions in Ireland, UK, Europe, Australia, New Zealand, Canada and the US. His productions for Fishamble have won many Irish and international awards, including an Olivier Award for *Silent* by Pat Kinevane. He has also directed for the Abbey Theatre, Woodpecker/Gaiety, 7:84 (Scotland), Project, Amharclann de híde, Tinderbox, Passion Machine, the Ark, Second Age, RTÉ Radio 1, the Belgrade, TNL Canada, Dundee Rep, Draíocht, TCD, Frontline Defenders, Amnesty International, Fighting Words, CoisCéim/Crash Ensemble/

GIAF, RTÉ lyric FM, APA and Vessel (Australia), Solas Nua and Kennedy Center (Washington DC), Odyssey (LA), and Irish Arts Center, Origin/1st Irish, 59E59 and IAC/Symphony Space Broadway (New York). Jim has taught for NYU, NUIM, GSA, Uversity, the Lir, Notre Dame, UM, Villanova, UMD, TCD and UCD.

Karen Ardiff was born in Dublin and graduated from the Samuel Beckett Centre in TCD. Karen's previous work with Fishamble includes *Inside the GPO* (2016) and *Rathmines Road* by Deirdre Kinahan (2018). Karen's most recent screen appearances include the Oscar-nominated *Brooklyn* directed by John Crowley as well as RTE's *Acceptable Risk*. Other previous film/TV includes *The Bookshop* (Isabel Coixet), *Noble* (nominated for several international awards and 3 IFTAs), *A Terrible Beauty...* (Tile Films) as well as *Evelyn*. Karen most recently appeared on stage in the highly successful show *The Unmanageable Sisters* on the Abbey Stage in the leading role of Rose. Other recent stage credits include: *Normal* (Maisie Lee, WeGetHighonthisCollective), *Angela's Ashes* (Thom Sutherland, Bord Gáis Energy Theatre), *Oedipus* (Wayne Jordan, The Abbey Theatre), *Peer Gynt* (Lynne Parker, Rough Magic – Irish Times Best Supporting Actress nomination), *Threepenny Opera* (Wayne Jordan, The Gate Theatre) *Steel Magnolias* (The Gaiety Theatre), and *Love in the Title* (Abbey/International tour – ESB/Irish Times Best Actress Award). Work with other companies includes: *The Colleen Bawn* (Bedrock – Irish Times Best Supporting Actress nomination), *The Stuff of Myth* (Crazy Dog Audio Theatre & Lane Productions) and Helene Hannf in *84 Charing Cross Road* (Andrews Lane Theatre – Irish Times Best Actress nomination for both). Karen has also performed in numerous radio dramas including *Duet* (Newstalk*), Tempting Faith* and *Greed is Good* (BBC4).

Lorcan Cranitch began working in the early 1980s in theatre in the UK. He has been busy on both sides of the Irish Sea ever since. In Dublin, he has worked mainly at the Abbey and Gate theatres, in plays by Tom Murphy, Brian Friel, Frank McGuinness, Arthur Miller, Shakespeare, Oscar Wilde and Chekhov. In the UK, he has worked with major repertory companies, the Royal Shakespeare Company, the National Theatre and the West End. His film and television work includes,

The Dig, Dancing at Lughnasa, Ballykissangel, Waking the Dead, Spooks, Omagh, ROME, Shackleton, and *Cracker.*

Maeve Fitzgerald is a graduate of the Bachelor in Acting Studies at the Samuel Beckett Centre, Trinity College. Maeve most recently appeared as Beatrice in *Much Ado About Nothing* for Rough Magic at the Kilkenny Arts Festival (2019). Other recent theatre includes: *The Thing About December* and *The Mai* (Decadent Theatre), *Wringer* (Bewley's Cafe Theatre), *On Raftery's Hill* (Abbey Theatre – nominee Best Actress Irish Times Theatre Awards 2019), *Holy Mary* (Breda Cashe Productions), *Bailegangaire* (Livin' Dred/Nomad). Maeve has also appeared in various productions for The Gate Theatre, Verdant Productions, Tron Theatre, ANU, Tall Tales, Second Age and many others. She won the Best Supporting Actress award for *Basin* and was nominated as Best Actress for *After Miss Julie*, both at the Irish Times Theatre Awards 2010.

Fionntán Larney is a writer and performer from Dublin. Last year, Fionntán graduated from The Lir Academy and wrote *beat*, which premiered at the Dublin Fringe Festival, before transferring to the Samuel Beckett Theatre for an extended run, and receiving a Fishamble New Writing Award nomination. Acting credits include: *Travesty* (The New Theatre), *The Lost O'Casey* (ANU/Abbey/Gate Theatre) and *The Metals* (Dublin Theatre Festival).

Rory Nolan's previous work with Fishamble includes *GPO 1818*. His theatre credits include *DruidShakespeare: Richard III, Shelter, Waiting for Godot, DruidShakespeare: Richard II, Henry IV (Pts 1&2), Henry V, The Colleen Bawn, DruidMurphy – Plays by Tom Murphy* (Druid); *Northern Star, The Critic, Peer Gynt, The Importance of Being Earnest, Don Carlos, The Taming of the Shrew, Improbable Frequency, Is This About Sex?* (Rough Magic); *Chekhov's First Play* (Dead Centre); *Postcards from the Ledge, Breaking Dad, Between Foxrock and a Hard Place, The Last Days of the Celtic Tiger, Sleeping Beauty* (Landmark Productions); *The Importance of Being Earnest, Bedroom Farce, A Christmas Carol, Death of a Salesman* (Gate Theatre); *She Stoops to Conquer, Aristocrats, The Government Inspector, Translations, Arrah Na Pogue, Macbeth, The Rivals, Last Days of a Reluctant Tyrant, The Comedy of Errors, Heavenly Bodies, Big Love* (Abbey Theatre); *Observe the Sons of Ulster Marching*

Towards the Somme (Livin' Dred/Nomad); *Cat on a Hot Tin Roof* (Corn Exchange); *The Evils of Tobacco* (Mangiare Theatre). Film & television includes: *Acceptable Risk, The Delinquent Season, WILD, Charlie, Fair City, A Thousand Times Goodnight, The Baker Street Irregulars, Trouble in Paradise, Nothing Personal.* Awards: Irish Times Irish Theatre Award for Best Supporting Actor (*Waiting for Godot*).

Rachel O'Byrne's theatre credits include *The Mai* (Decadent Theatre Company); *Assassins, The Great Gatsby* (2017, 2018/19), *One for the Road, The Constant Wife* (Gate Theatre); *The Good Father, At the Ford* (Rise Productions); *The Sin Eaters* (ANU Productions); *The Remains of Maisie Duggan, By the Bog of Cats* (Abbey Theatre); *Brigit* (Druid); *Othello* (Theatre Royal). Film credits include *Mammal* (Fastnet Films) and *Kaleidoscope* (The Lir Academy). Rachel trained at The Lir Academy and holds a BA in Drama and French from Trinity College Dublin.

Arthur Riordan is an actor and playwright. Arthur last worked with Fishamble on the Irish, UK and Australia tour of *Swing.* Other recent stage appearances include *A Day* (Olympia Theatre); *From Under the Bed* (Big Guerrilla Productions); *Krapp's Last Tape* (Theatre Royal, Waterford); *Kings of the Kilburn High Road* with Livin' Dred/Verdant productions. He has also worked extensively with Rough Magic (of which he is a founder member), as well as many other leading Irish theatre companies, including the Abbey and Peacock, Druid, Gaiety, Corcadorca, and Pan Pan. Arthur has also made numerous television and film appearances, including *Out of Here, Ripper Street, Stella Days, Killinaskully, The Tudors, Fair City, The Clinic, The Baker Street Irregulars, The Chosen, Borstal Boy, Rat, The Last September,* and *Pitch n' Putt with Beckett n' Joyce.* Arthur's writing includes the stage adaptation *of A Portrait of the Artist as a Young Man,* libretto for Andrew Synnott's opera *Dubliners* for Opera Theatre Company, book and lyrics for the hit musical *The Train,* an adaptation of Ibsen's *Peer Gynt,* book and lyrics for the multi-award-winning hit musical *Improbable Frequency* and a one-man show, *The Emergency Session* (all for Rough Magic); a stage adaptation of Flann O'Brien's *Slattery's Sago Saga* (for The Performance Corporation); *Love Me?!* (for The Corn Exchange); and two collaborations with Des Bishop

– *Rap Eire* (for Bickerstaffe), and *Shooting Gallery* (for Bedrock Productions).

Maree Kearns has previously designed *Rathmines Road, Maz and Bricks* and *Invitation to a Journey* (a CoisCeim/Crash Ensemble coproduction) for Fishamble. Recent designs include *Two Pints* at the Abbey Theatre, *Torch* for Anu Productions and *The Odd Couple* at the Everyman. Other work includes *Class* for Inis Theatre (Edinburgh Fringe First 2018), *The Wizard of Oz* at the Cork Opera House, *Agnes, Pageant* and *Faun* for CoisCeim, *Giselle* for Ballet Ireland, *Annie the Musical* and *ProdiJIG the Revolution* for Cork Opera House, *Desire Under The Elms* for Corn Exchange, *Monsters, Dinosaurs and Ghosts* at the Peacock, *These Halcyon Days* for Landmark & Tall Tales, *Zoe's Play* and *Far Away From Me* at The Ark**,** *Hamlet, King Lear, Romeo and Juliet, Macbeth* and *Dancing at Lughnasa* for Second Age, *Moll* and *Anglo the Musical* for Verdant Productions, *Plasticine* for Corcadorca, *Bronte, A Winter's Tale, Three Winters, In the Next Room, Scenes from the Big Picture* and *Troilus and Cressida* for the Lir. Maree has been the recipient of an Irish Times Theatre Award for her design of *Observe the Sons of Ulster Marching Towards the Somme* and is the course Director for the Masters in Theatre Design at the Lir Academy in Dublin.

Mark Galione's designs for Fishamble: The New Play Company most recently include *On Blueberry Hill, Swing,* and *Inside The GPO*. His designs in Ireland include works for Irish Modern Dance Theatre, CoisCéim, Dance Theatre of Ireland, The Peacock, Fíbín, Hands Turn, Classic Stage Ireland, Barabbas, Vesuvius, The Derry Playhouse, The Ark, Peer to Peer, Gonzo, Theatre Lovett, Second Age Theatre Company, Barnstorm, and *I'm Your Man* for THISISPOPBABY. Recent TV includes *Jack Lukeman 27 Club, All Ireland Schools Talent Search,* TG4 – *Country Music Legends* and *The Al Porter Christmas Show RTE2*. Mark is a staff Lighting Designer at High Res Lighting.

Saileóg O'Halloran's theatre credits include *The Anvil* (Anu/ Manchester International Festival), *The Bluffer's Guide to Suburbia* (Once Off Productions/Cork Midsummer Festival), *The Misfits* (Corn Exchange), *Macnas 2018, Copperface Jacks the Musical* (Verdant), *GPO 1818* (Fishamble), *The Half of It* (MOMMO), *The Shitstorm* (Dublin Fringe), *The Seagull* (Corn Exchange), *To Hell In A Handbag* (Show In A Bag/Tiger Dublin

Fringe), *Town is Dead* (Peacock Theatre), *Embodied* (Dublin Dance Festival), *Shibboleth* (Peacock Theatre), *Chekhov's First Play* (Dead Centre), *Thirteen* (Irish Times Judges Special Award – ANU Productions) and *Wake* (Chamber Made Opera). Film and television credits include *Bainne* (Anabasis Films), *Cynthia* (Copper Alley Productions) *Procession* (925 Productions), *The Trap* (Treasure Entertainment), *Away With The Fairies* (Treasure Entertainment), *Pebbles* (Jonathan Shaw Dir), *Lost in the Living* (Ballyrogan Films), *Children of the Revolution* (RTÉ), and *The Inquiry* (DCTV).

Denis Clohessy has worked with numerous dance and theatre companies including Fishamble, The Abbey Theatre, The Gate Theatre, Rough Magic, Junk Ensemble, Corn Exchange, The Tron Theatre, Glasgow, Northlight Theatre, Chicago and Beijing Children's Art Theatre. He won the Irish Times Theatre Award for Best Design Sound in 2011 (for Rough Magic's *Sodome, My Love)*, he was a nominee in 2015 (for Junk Ensemble and Brokentalker's *It Folds*), was an associate artist with the Abbey in 2008, and was a participant on Rough Magic's ADVANCE programme in 2012. In 2016, Pat Kinevane's play *Silent* (Fishamble) for which Denis composed the music won an Olivier Award. His work in Film and Television includes music for the feature films *Under The Clock* and *Older than Ireland* (Snackbox Films), *The Irish Pub* (Atom Films), *His and Hers* (Venom Film), *The Land of the Enlightened* (Savage Film), *In View* (Underground Cinema), *The Reluctant Revolutionary* (Underground Films) and the television series *The Limits of Liberty* (South Wind Blows) performed by the RTÉ Concert Orchestra.

Oisín Kearney is a writer, director and filmmaker. He trained in television production in the *Aim High* scheme run by BBC NI, NI Screen and Skillset. He was Associate Producer on Oscar-long-listed and Emmy-nominated *ELIÁN* and Assistant Producer on Irish box-office hit *66 DAYS*. His credits as a film director include *All For Show* (BBC NI True North), *Bbeyond* (BBC Arts Show), *Borderlands* and *Unfinished Revolution* (De Correspondent, NPO2), and *BOJAYÁ: Caught In The Crossfire* (Hot Docs Film Festival 2019).

Marie Tierney is a production manager, she has toured extensively both nationally and internationally. Recent credits include *Haughey Gregory, On Blueberry Hill* and *Rathmines Road* for Fishamble: The New Play Company, *Ulysses* for The Abbey Theatre, *The Only Jealousy of Emer* for Dublin City Arts Office and The Nigerian Carnival, and she has been production manager for The Gap Arts Festival for the past 8 years. She has coordinated many large scale and site-specific productions. Previously she has been design coordinator on many productions such as St Patricks Festival, Special Olympics opening ceremony, a number of site specific shows in swimming pools with Big Telly, and shows in Kilmainham Gaol.

As a film designer, she designed costumes for *Borstal Boy, Mapmaker, Crushproof, The Disappearance of Finbar, On Home Ground* for RTÉ and many Filmbase shorts. She designed set and costumes for *Kathleen Lynn: The Rebel Doctor* and *James Gandon: A Life* for Loopline films.

She is course director on Colaiste Dhulaigh's Performing Arts course and she delivers modules in technical theatre and design.

She is a member of the board of directors of the Association of Irish Stage Technicians, which promotes safety and training in the arts.

Sarah Keane is a production manager and began her career in theatre as an ASM and Stage Manager. She then worked as a technician for Project Arts Centre during their time at Project@ the mint. From there she joined the Civic Theatre as Assistant Technical Manager where she spent the last 20 years working on countless productions with companies from all over the world, including several Fishamble productions over the years. This is her first time working directly with Fishamble.

Fiona Keller's recent credits as Stage Manager include *The Patient Gloria* by Gina Moxley and Abbey Theatre with Pan Pan (Fringe First and Herald Angel winner), and *Theatre For One* (Landmark Productions and Cork Midsummer Festival). *Lost O'Casey, Sin Eaters, Sunder, Vardo, Thirteen, Boys of Foley Street* all with ANU. *These Rooms* (CoisCéim and ANU), *RTE's Reflecting The Rising* (RTÉ and ANU), *On Corporation Street* (HOME Manchester and ANU Productions). *Chekhov's First Play* and *Lippy* (Dead Centre), *This Beach* (Brokentalkers), *Alive! Awake!* and *The Summoning* (Macnas).

Sarah Purcell is a theatre studies graduate of Colaiste Dhulaigh College of Further Education. Some of her previous ASM credits include: *Copper Face Jacks: the Musical* (Verdant 2019), *Haughey|Gregory* (Fishamble 2019), *Aladdin* (Cork Opera House 2019), *Rathmines Road* (Fishamble 2018), *The Wizard of Oz* (Cork Opera House 2018), *My Son, My Son* (Project Arts Centre 2018), *Snow White and the Seven Dwarfs* (Cork Opera House 2018), *The Chastitute* (Gaiety Theatre 2017), *Cinderella* (Cork Opera House 2017), *ProdiJIG* (Cork Opera House 2016), *Signatories* (Verdant Productions in association with UCD 2016), *Kings of the Kilburn High Road* (Livin' Dred 2016), *Freezin'* (Olympia Theatre 2016), *Are You There Garth? It's Me, Margaret* (Pat Egan Productions 2016), *The Bloody Irish!* (Bloody Irish Productions DAC 2015), *The Field, Moll* (Verdant Productions) and has stage managed *To Hell in a Handbag* which originated as a *Show in a Bag* in Dublin Fringe 2016.

Martha Fitzgerald is a Dublin based theatre maker who has just completed the MA in Theatre Practice at the Gaiety School of Acting and UCD. She is the co-founder of Fizz and Chips Theatre Company.

Gavin Kostick, as literary manager at Fishamble, works with new writers for theatre through script development, readings and a variety of mentorship programmes. For Fishamble Gavin is particularly proud of his work on *Show in a Bag, The New Play Clinic, Tiny Plays for Ireland* and *A Play for Ireland*. Gavin is also an award-winning playwright. He has written over twenty plays which have been produced nationally and internationally. Recent favourite works include, *Invitation to a Journey* and *The End of the Road* for Fishamble, *This is What we Sang* for Kabosh, *Fight Night, The Games People Play* and *At the Ford* for RISE and the Libretto for *The Alma Fetish* for Raymond Deane and Wide Open Opera. As a performer he performed Joseph Conrad's *Heart of Darkness: Complete*, a six hour show for Absolut Fringe, Dublin Theatre Festival and The London Festival of Literature at the Southbank. His work in all areas has received many national and international awards.

Eva Scanlan is the general manager and producer of Fishamble: The New Play Company. Current and recent producing work includes *Before* by Pat Kinevane, *Rathmines Road* by Deirdre Kinahan, *Haughey|Gregory* by Colin Murphy, *On Blueberry Hill* by Sebastian Barry, Fishamble's award-winning Pat Kinevane Trilogy on tour in Ireland and internationally, *The Humours of Bandon* by Margaret McAuliffe, *Maz and Bricks* by Eva O'Connor, *Inside the GPO* by Colin Murphy, *Tiny Plays for Ireland and America* and *Swing* on tour in Ireland, the UK, and Australia. Eva produces *The 24 Hour Plays: Dublin* at the Abbey Theatre in Ireland (2012–present), in association with the 24 Hour Play Company, New York, and has worked on The 24 Hour Plays on Broadway and The 24 Hour Musicals at the Gramercy Theatre. Previously, she was Producer of terraNOVA Collective in New York (2012–2015).

ABOUT FISHAMBLE: THE NEW PLAY COMPANY

'Ireland's leading new writing company'
THE STAGE

Fishamble is passionate about discovering, developing and producing new plays.

It is named after the Playhouse on Dublin's Fishamble Street which, in the 1780s, became the first theatre to commission and produce plays by Irish writers.

'Fishamble puts electricity in the National Grid of dreams'
SEBASTIAN BARRY

Fishamble believes that vibrant theatre stands at the centre of a vibrant civic society. It harnesses the imaginative power of theatre to provide audiences with a diverse range of contemporary, compelling and heartfelt dramatic works.

'A global brand with international theatrical presence'
THE IRISH TIMES

Fishamble thinks nationally and reaches globally. It works collaboratively with networks of artists, communities, and organisations, to achieve the maximum possible life for its plays. For instance, over 30 Fishamble playscripts have been published.

Fishamble has toured its productions to audiences throughout Ireland, and to 19 other countries. It typically produces over 200 performances annually, from the Aran Islands to Auckland, Ballymun to Brisbane, Clonmel to Cleveland.

'Forward-thinking Fishamble'
THE NEW YORK TIMES

Fishamble champions the role of the playwright, through its productions, and wide range of artist support and development initiatives. It works with over 50% of the writers of all new plays produced on the island of Ireland each year.

'Excellent Fishamble... Ireland's terrific Fishamble'
THE GUARDIAN

Fishamble has received many awards in Ireland and internationally, including an Olivier Award, won jointly with Pat Kinevane. Its living archive is at the National Library of Ireland.

'When Fishamble is [in New York], you've got to go'
TIME OUT NEW YORK

FISHAMBLE'S RECENT AND CURRENT
PRODUCTIONS INCLUDE:

- On *Blueberry Hill* by Sebastian Barry (2017–19) touring in Ireland, Europe, and Off-Broadway

- *Before* by Pat Kinevane (2018–19) touring in association with the Strollers Network, and internationally

- *Haughey|Gregory* by Colin Murphy (2018–19) in the Abbey Theatre, Mountjoy Prison, Dáil Éireann, Croke Park, and Larkin Community College, as well as on national tour with the Nasc Network

- *The Humours of Bandon* by Margaret McAuliffe (2017–19) touring in Ireland, UK, US, and Australia

- *Rathmines* Road by Deirdre Kinahan (2018) in coproduction with the Abbey Theatre

- *Drip Feed* by Karen Cogan (2018) in coproduction with Soho Theatre, touring in Ireland and UK

- *GPO 1818* by Colin Murphy (2018) to mark the bicentenary of the GPO

- *Maz & Bricks* by Eva O'Connor (2017–18) on national and international tour

- *Forgotten, Silent* and *Underneath* by Pat Kinevane (since 2007, 2011 and 2014, respectively – 2018) touring in Ireland, UK, Europe, US, Australia and New Zealand

- *Charolais* by Noni Stapleton (2017) in New York

- *Inside the GPO* by Colin Murphy (2016) performed in the GPO during Easter

- *Tiny Plays for Ireland and America* by 26 writers (2016) at the Kennedy Center, Washington DC, and Irish Arts Center, New York, as part of *Ireland 100*

- *Mainstream* by Rosaleen McDonagh (2016) in coproduction with Project Arts Centre

- *Invitation to a Journey* by David Bolger, Deirdre Gribbin and Gavin Kostick (2016) in coproduction with CoisCeim, Crash Ensemble and Galway International Arts Festival

- *Little Thing, Big Thing* by Donal O'Kelly (2014–16) touring in Ireland, UK, Europe, US and Australia

- *Swing* by Steve Blount, Peter Daly, Gavin Kostick and Janet Moran (2014–16) touring in Ireland, UK, Europe, US, Australia and New Zealand

- *Spinning* by Deirdre Kinahan (2014) at Dublin Theatre Festival

- *The Wheelchair on My Face* by Sonya Kelly (2013–14) touring in Ireland, UK, Europe and US.

Fishamble Staff: Jim Culleton (Artistic Director), Eva Scanlan (General Manager and Producer), Gavin Kostick (Literary Manager), Chandrika Narayanan-Mohan (Marketing and Development Manager), Ronan Carey (Office and Production Coordinator).

Fishamble Board: Tania Banotti, Padraig Burns, Peter Finnegan, Louise Molloy, Doireann Ní Bhriain (Chair), Vincent O'Doherty, John O'Donnell, Siobhan O'Leary, Andrew Parkes.

THE PROCESS OF A PLAY FOR IRELAND

In 2011, Fishamble invited submissions of tiny plays, and received over 1,700 submissions. *Tiny Plays for Ireland* subsequently played to sell out runs in Ireland, transferred to the Kennedy Center and Irish Arts Center in the US as part of *Ireland 100*, generated similar initiatives in the US, Australia and Russia, and was called 'a brilliant project...really wonderful' by President Higgins.

In 2017, inspired by the public's appetite for work that really engaged with contemporary concerns, Fishamble launched a call for ideas for one, big, ambitious play – a play for Ireland. A work that would capture the zeitgeist of the country. Fishamble received over 370 proposals. *A Play for Ireland [APFI]* was designed as a two-year artist development initiative to mentor playwrights throughout the island of Ireland, and result in the production of a very special new play. The initiative has been run in partnership with six venues across the country: Draíocht, The Everyman, Lime Tree Theatre/Belltable, Lyric Theatre, Pavilion Theatre, and Town Hall Theatre. It has been supported by the Arts Council, and by sponsors Irish Rail and Tesco Finest.

In April 2018, Fishamble and the partner venues chose five ideas to develop through the initiative in each venue, making a total of 30 plays, to mark Fishamble's 30th year. It has been a huge privilege to work with wonderful playwrights during this time: Ann Blake, Mike Finn, Brendan Griffin, Michael Hilliard Mulcahy, and Joanne Ryan in Lime Tree Theatre/Belltable; Caitríona Daly, Jeda de Brí & Finbarr Doyle, Barry McStay, Alice Murphy, and Ian Toner in Draíocht; Noelle Brown & Karen Cogan, Lisa Carroll, John Doran, Bridgid Galvin, and Margaret McAuliffe in The Everyman; Vittoria Cafolla, Seamus Collins, Clare McMahon, Michael Patrick & Oisín Kearney, and Shannon Sickels (Yee) at Lyric Theatre; David Horan, Shay Linehan, Jody O'Neill, Lee Stafford, and Ciara Elizabeth Smyth at Pavilion Theatre; Fionn Foley, Janet Moran, Marina Ní Dhubháin, Neasa O'Callaghan, and Hugh Travers in Town Hall Theatre.

During April–November 2018, the playwrights met at each venue, to discuss and develop their plays, with Jim Culleton and Gavin Kostick from Fishamble, and guest directors and designers, including Annabelle Comyn, Oonagh Murphy, Lynne Parker, Maree Kearns, Niamh Lunny, and Saileóg O'Halloran. At the end of 2018, a draft was submitted of the plays.

In February 2019, one writer from each venue was chosen by Fishamble and the venues, and these six shortlisted plays were optioned by Fishamble. They were: *Duck, Duck, Goose* by Caitríona Daly (Draíocht); *In Passing* by John Doran (The Everyman); *Wreckquiem* by Mike Finn (Lime Tree Theatre/ Belltable); *A Line of Work* by Marina Ni Dhubháin (Town Hall Theatre); *Ballybaile* by Jody O'Neill (Pavilion Theatre); *The Alternative* by Michael Patrick & Oisín Kearney (Lyric Theatre).

The shortlisted plays were developed further through readings and discussions with a team of actors: Karen Ardiff, Steve Blount, Tara Breathnach, Kate Brennan, Emmet Byrne, Lorcan Crannitch, John Doran, Clare Dunne, Maeve Fitzgerald, Fionn Foley, Michele Forbes, Ali Fox, Eanna Hardwicke, Katie Honan, Fionntán Larney, Ronan Leahy, Julie Maguire, Karen McCartney, Michael Glenn Murphy, Kate Murray, Mary Murray, Rory Nolan, Marion O'Dwyer, Mark O'Regan, David Pearse, Roseanna Purcell, Bryan Quinn, Arthur Riordan, Kieran Roche, Joan Sheehy, Pat Shortt and Amilia Stewart.

In March 2019, a subsequent draft was submitted, and *APFI* was chosen from these drafts. The Fishamble team, and the partner judges, were joined for this part of the process by independent assessor, international dramaturg Ruth Little.

In April 2019, *The Alternative* became the chosen play and was commissioned and developed further by Fishamble, up to its rehearsals in August. The production was produced by Fishamble, in partnership with the partner venues, and toured to all these venues in September/October 2019.

Fishamble wishes to thank the following Friends of Fishamble & Corporate Members for their invaluable support:

Alan & Rosemary Ashe, ATM Accounting Services, Mary Banotti, Tania Banotti, Doireann Ní Bhriain, Conor Braiden, Business to Arts, Breda Cashe, Maura Connolly, John & Yvonne Healy, Gillie Hinds, Monica McInerney, Stuart Mclaughlin, Ger McNaughton,

Sinead Moriarty, Pat Moylan, Dympna Murray, Liz Nugent, Lisney, Vincent O'Doherty, Nora Owen, David & Veronica Rowe, Mary Stephenson, Patrick Sutton, and Tesco Finest. Thank you also to all those who do not wish to be credited.

fishamble.com

facebook.com/fishamble

twitter.com/fishamble

Fishamble is funded by The Arts Council and Dublin City Council. Its international touring is supported by Culture Ireland.

ACKNOWLEDGEMENTS

Thanks to the following for their help with this production:
Rachel West and David Parnell and all at the Arts Council; Ray
Yeates and all at Dublin City Council Arts Office; Christine
Sisk, Ciaran Walsh, Valerie Behan and all at Culture Ireland;
Louise Donlon, Marketa Dowling, and all at Lime Tree Theatre/
Belltable; Fergal McGrath and all at Town Hall Theatre; Jimmy
Fay, Rebecca Mairs, and all at the Lyric Theatre; Emer McGowan
and all at Draíocht; Hugh Murray, Niall O'Connell, and all
at Pavilion Theatre; Julie Kelleher and all at The Everyman;
Ruth Little; Laura MacNaughton, Aoife McCollum and all at
the O'Reilly Theatre; all at 3 Great Denmark Street; Eoghan
Carrick; O'Reilly Theatre; Colm Maher; Colm O'Kane; Kate
Campbell; Ursula Lysaght (for letting us use her name); Mobile
Radio Links; the Olympia Theatre and the Abbey Theatre; Irish
Rail; Tesco Finest; Ciara Elizabeth Smyth, Naomi Sheehan,
Patrick McBrearty, Mary McGurk, Holly Hannaway, Stefan
Dunbar, Emma Jordan, Caoileann Curry Thompson, Pete
Graham, Federico Rea, Chris Scott, Eoin Kilkenny, Dr Conor
Mulvagh, Dr John Gallagher; Colm Maher; all those who have
helped since this publication went to print.

To the people of Ireland.

CHARACTERS LIST

RICHARD DEVLIN *(BBC Producer, Grainne's father)*
GRAINNE DEVLIN *(Physics Student, Richard's daughter)*
JOHN FITZGIBBON *(BBC Debate Presenter)*
HANNAH MURRAY *(BBC Assistant Producer)*
URSULA LYSAGHT *(Prime Minister of The United Kingdom of Great Britain and Ireland)*
PETER KEOGH *(Irish First Minister and Leader of the Irish Parliamentary Party)*
PATRICK *(Vote Leave protestor)*

Three members of the audience will be given cards and asked to read the lines for:

QUESTIONER 1
QUESTIONER 2
QUESTIONER 3

FILMED CHARACTERS

NIAMH *(Richard's dead wife, Grainne's dead mother)*
REPORTER
VOX POP 1
VOX POP 2
VOX POP 3
VOX POP 4
VOX POP 5
PRESENTERS *(Voice over only)*

ANNOUNCEMENTS

EVERYMAN

ANNOUNCER Welcome to the Royal Everyman Theatre.[1]

Please stand for our National Anthem.

PAVILION

ANNOUNCER Welcome to the Pavilion Theatre, Kingstown.[2]

Please stand for our National Anthem.

BELLTABLE

ANNOUNCER Welcome to the King George Theatre[3] Limerick.

Please stand for our National Anthem.

TOWN HALL

ANNOUNCER Welcome to the Royal Court Theatre,[4] Galway.

Please stand for our National Anthem.

---

[1] The Everyman Theatre was built in 1897. This renaming as the 'Royal Everyman Theatre' highlights a link to the British Royal family in alternative reality.

[2] The Pavilion Theatre is in the Irish town of Dún Laoghaire. It was renamed Kingstown in honour of King George IV's 1821 visit, before reverting to its original name upon Irish independence.

[3] Belltable Limerick is found on O'Connell Street. This street was originally Geoge's Street, before it was renamed after Daniel O'Connell.

[4] The building which houses the Town Hall Theatre was erected in the 1820s and served first as a courthouse. This is also a reference to the Royal Court Theatre in London.

DRAÍOCHT

ANNOUNCER Welcome to the Prince's Theatre, Blanchardstown.[5]

Please stand for our National Anthem.

LYRIC

ANNOUNCER Welcome to the Dame Mary O'Malley Memorial Theatre.[6]

Please stand for our National Anthem.

---

[5] Draíocht Arts Centre, Blanchardstown has been renamed as the 'Prince's Theatre' to highlight a link to the British Royal family in alternative reality.
[6] Mary O'Malley was a theatre director who founded The Belfast Lyric Players, later becoming the Lyric Theatre. She was not a Dame.

ACT ONE

Scene One

A screen lights up. A full choir sings one chorus of **'GOD SAVE THE QUEEN'** *as Gaeilge.*

Video archive of the last one hundred years of Irish history in this universe.

DIA LENÁR BHANRÍON
ÁR BHANRÍON GO DEO
DIA LENÁR BHANRÍON
SEOL LEIS AN BUA Í
RÍMÉAD AGUS GLÓR UIRTHI,
AGUS MUID FAOI REIM TAMALL FADA,
DIA LENÁR BHANRÍON[7]

BBC Dublin studio. Shiny floor. Cameras. Wires and studio equipment. Flightcases.

A staircase on one side leads up to the production office which overlooks the studio floor. On one side

---

[7] The national anthem of the United Kingdom of Great Britain and Northern Ireland.

God Save the Queen in Irish:

God save our gracious Queen,
Long live our noble Queen,
God save the Queen;
Send her victorious,
Happy and glorious,
Long to reign over us,
God save the Queen.

is a gallery space with a mixing desk, at which sits a technician.

In the office, a desk and a bust of Oliver Cromwell.[8]

RICHARD *storms into the studio, followed by* **JOHN**.

JOHN *holds a Pret a Manger*[9] *coffee cup in one hand and a little white bag with a bagel in the other.* **RICHARD** *has a reusable glass coffee cup and a notebook.*

They walk and talk, heading up the staircase into the office.

JOHN Four pound fifty![10]

RICHARD Yep.

JOHN Four pound fifty for a coffee!

RICHARD I know.

JOHN Four pound fucking fifty for a fucking cup of coffee Richard?!

RICHARD I / know!

JOHN What is Dublin coming to? It's getting like fucking Zurich!

RICHARD Not like you can't afford it.

JOHN It's not even the good stuff.

HANNAH *crosses the studio, carrying papers, with her phone held between her ear and her shoulder.*

HANNAH Yeah yeah yeah, grand, yeah, lovely.

RICHARD You can tell the difference, can you?

---

[8] Oliver Cromwell is a hated figure in modern Ireland due to his military campaign in the Wars of the Three Kingdoms.

In the Cromwellian conquest of Ireland, there were 20,000–30,000 battlefield casualties, and 200,000–600,000 civilian casualties.

[9] Pret a Manger currently does not operate any shops on the island of Ireland.

[10] Ireland uses the Euro.

JOHN I can. D'ya know / in Milan...

> JOHN *and* RICHARD *reach the top of the staircase and enter the office.* HANNAH *climbs the staircase, and shouts after them, having hung up her phone.*

HANNAH The Prime Minister's on her way!

RICHARD How long Hannah?

HANNAH About 15 minutes.

JOHN She was in my History class at uni/ you know.

RICHARD Any sign of Keogh yet?

HANNAH Not yet.

> HANNAH *enters the office. She hands some of the papers to* RICHARD.

RICHARD Right, what have we got?

HANNAH These are the new run-downs.

JOHN Used to be in the Trinity Young Conservatives.

> HANNAH *hands some papers to* JOHN *and checks her phone for updates.*

RICHARD They reviewed the format?

HANNAH We did a walk-through with their staff earlier.

JOHN And now she's Labour's saviour.

HANNAH The PM wants the handshake nearer the audience.

RICHARD Grand.

JOHN She was stuck up, even back then.

RICHARD The gallery happy? Elaine yapping away?

HANNAH No more than usual.

JOHN Fond of auld 'sneachta bán'.[11]

---

[11] Cocaine. Literally 'White Snow' in the Irish language.

RICHARD John, please. Set ready?

HANNAH Podiums are prepped.

JOHN You should see our sting for the top of the show, Rich. Some fancy jiggery-pokery from the graphics guys.

HANNAH And here's all the latest polls.

JOHN You'd never know we were bankrupt.

HANNAH Including that Ipsos-MORI[12] one.

RICHARD What about it?

HANNAH *hands him another print-out.*

HANNAH The one with Leave ahead.

RICHARD Bloody hell.

He pours over the poll.

JOHN An eleventh hour surge.

RICHARD She should never have called this bloody referendum. What do the other polls say?

HANNAH They still have Remain ahead, but they're tight.

JOHN Exciting.

RICHARD *This* is why she decided to come at the last minute.

HANNAH They must have similar internals.

JOHN They should have stuck with Kendrick. He's a terrible Chancellor, but he can make the economic argument!

RICHARD *(gesturing to the paper)* It's clearly not working.

JOHN The Prime Minister returning to her hometown to save the Union! She's desperate.

RICHARD Better optics than cowering in Downing street.

---

[12] Ipsos MORI is a market research company in the United Kingdom. It is a member of the British Polling Council.

JOHN Well, it's certainly dramatic.

HANNAH Oh and Keogh's put out a statement on the Prime Minister coming over.

JOHN Making a play for the country.

HANNAH Saying she only comes to Ireland when her paycheck's in danger.

JOHN A play for Ireland.

HANNAH And he's accused us of having an agenda.

JOHN Well, we are the *British* Broadcasting Company.

RICHARD *Corporation* John. Jesus you've only been working here ten years. Are the questions sorted?

HANNAH *shuffles through her papers.*

HANNAH Yes. We can do four between each of the ad breaks.

JOHN Thank God they abolished the licence fee.[13]

RICHARD Like you ever paid it anyway. Give us the questions there.

HANNAH Are you sure you can get across these in time Rich? You know I'm ready.

RICHARD Questions Hannah.

HANNAH *receives a phone-call.*

HANNAH They're on my laptop. Give me a second. *(Into phone)* Hello?

HANNAH *leaves the office, walks down the stairs and offstage.*

RICHARD How's she been?

---

[13] Instead of adverts, the BBC in the UK is funded by a Licence Fee, which is required to be paid if you watch live television.

JOHN Ah, thinks she's the big producer now. A bit too much of this *(gestures chit-chat with his hand)*. But everyone in the gallery loves her. You're lucky you were allowed back in.

RICHARD I've taught her well.

> **JOHN** *pulls out his avocado, bacon, and egg bagel and begins eating it.*

Do you have to do that now, John?

JOHN Rich, I've been working twenty hours a day! I apologise if my eating habits do not please you. *(Pause)* So as I was saying...in Milan, you can get a world-class espresso for one euro. And in the CAS, I had this gorgeous stuff for about thirty cents! That's under twenty pence! Dublin? *(Holds coffee aloft)* Four hundred and fifty of the Queen's pence.

RICHARD When were you in the Central America States?[14]

JOHN Oh, years ago. Martha and I honeymooned in Playa Grande. It means 'big beach'. We went to see the turtles breeding.

RICHARD What?

JOHN Hundreds of these leatherbacks. Big fuck off bastards.

RICHARD You went to watch turtles get the ride?

JOHN We did.

RICHARD On your honeymoon?

JOHN That's right.

RICHARD Was it any use?

---

[14] The Federal Republic of Central America was a sovereign state in Central America consisting of the territories of the former Captaincy General of Guatemala of New Spain. It existed from 1823 to 1841. At the end of World War II, interest in integrating the Central American governments began. On October 14, 1951 the governments of Costa Rica, El Salvador, Guatemala, Honduras and Nicaragua signed a treaty creating the Organization of Central American States to promote regional cooperation and unity.

JOHN No. The cunts do it at night. At high tide. So you can't see a fucking thing! We were sold a lie. Mmm, that's good bagel!

HANNAH *enters the office, carrying her laptop and a ream of papers.*

HANNAH John, can you please start getting ready? We're letting the audience in soon.

JOHN Just because I don't buzz about the building like a blue-arsed fly, doesn't mean I'm not working.

JOHN *takes another bite of his bagel.*

RICHARD *(noting the laptop)* You don't have print-outs, Hannah?

HANNAH Here.

HANNAH *quickly hands* **RICHARD** *some papers, he looks through them.*

John, please. Makeup's ready for you.

JOHN I was thinking I might go au-naturale tonight...

RICHARD John, I'm trying to catch up here.

JOHN Show off the true face of the nation.

RICHARD Hannah, what's this? Question 10. Carbon taxes?

HANNAH It's a legitimate issue. The Prime / Minister has –

RICHARD Yeah but not when the fate of the country's at stake.

HANNAH The fate of the world, Rich.

RICHARD I know that! I know you're on a crusade Hannah. And I'm doing my bit, I've got my reusable coffee cup for fuck sake!

HANNAH There was a story this week. Climate change has forced Maasi tribes in Tanzania to /abandon their traditional nomadic –

RICHARD Of course, of course – you care, I care, but the gluebags in Kingstown just want hotter summers.

JOHN Tonight is about Ireland, Hannah. Not the fucking Africans.

> RICHARD *flicks through the other questions.* HANNAH *receives a phone-call. She answers.*

HANNAH Hi Elaine...

RICHARD The people need the facts.

HANNAH Guest shot. Yeh. No worries.

RICHARD About the vote. Nothing else.

> HANNAH *hangs up.*

HANNAH Yeah yeah, you're right.

RICHARD And if it goes well, It won't go unnoticed.

JOHN The higher-ups will be watching.

> RICHARD *hands a pile of papers with questions on them to* HANNAH.

RICHARD The figures for the last programme looked good. Good work. For keeping things moving.

HANNAH Good work for dealing with Mr Celebrity you mean.

JOHN *(with mouthful of bagel)* I'm a respected journalist.

> HANNAH *gives* RICHARD *a look, and leaves.* JOHN *gestures the 'chit-chat' again to* RICHARD. *Through this dialogue,* RICHARD *is looking through papers, taking notes with a pen, and checking things on his laptop.* JOHN *is lounging, slurping his coffee.*

That poll's *very* interesting.

RICHARD It's a poll. It's not *that* interesting.

JOHN Might mix things up a bit.

RICHARD Perhaps you could hold it up.

JOHN Not only could I hold it up, I could quote from it.

RICHARD Double whammy!

JOHN Prop.

RICHARD Prop with a point!

> JOHN *rehearses holding up the poll and pointing at it.*

> I never thought I'd see the day that Irish people might vote to leave the UK.

JOHN No longer the United Kingdom of Great Britain and Ireland. Just 'Great Britain'.

RICHARD Or just '*Britain*'.

JOHN '*Britain*'. '*Britain*'. It's a very cold word isn't it? Hardly matches the warmth of the people at all.

RICHARD It won't happen.

JOHN Why not?

RICHARD Because we're British.

JOHN Yes. But. British or not, we Irish hate the English.

RICHARD We do.

JOHN We always have.

RICHARD It's hard not to.

> *Beat.*

> They *are* annoying.

JOHN It's their brashness.

RICHARD Their ignorance.

JOHN Their arrogance.

RICHARD Their sense of self-importance.

JOHN You'd never hear an Irishman go on about how great *his* country is!

RICHARD Never.

Beat.

JOHN You know, I didn't have a problem with them until I actually went to the mainland.[15] *(English accent)* 'Awww, I've never been to Ireland, but my granny's from Skibbereen.' Fuck 'em.

RICHARD Sure who would we be without our beloved English?

JOHN Right enough. And the Scots.

RICHARD And the Scots. And the Welsh.

JOHN And the Welsh. I always forget the Welsh.

RICHARD Poor man's Scot, the Welsh.

JOHN *(welsh accent)* 'Look at us with our dragons and our coal mines'. Couldn't even make it onto the Union Jack.[16] Cunts.

RICHARD We may hate the English, but we'll never leave them.

JOHN Sure that's the basis of my marriage.

RICHARD You hate Martha?

JOHN I love the woman! But *fuck* I hate her. It's complex. Much the same.

Beat. **RICHARD***'s pen has stopped working. He shakes it, tries it again and throws it down.*

How have you been coping?

---

[15] 'The mainland' is a phrase often used by Northern Irish Unionists to refer to Great Britain.
[16] The Union Jack consists of the Cross of St. George (England), St Andrew's Saltire (Scotland) and St. Patrick's Saltire (Ireland). It has no Welsh representation.

RICHARD *stops looking at papers. He looks at* JOHN, *takes a new pen out of his breast pocket and begins writing notes again.*

RICHARD Got to get on with it.

JOHN Are you sure you're up for tonight?

RICHARD Of course.

JOHN Rich, it's a well-oiled machine at this stage. Hannah could have handled it. And you know me. Sure, I'm great. You didn't need to come back in.

RICHARD I would have sat out the Chancellor, but there's no way I'm missing the Prime Minister.

JOHN I'm just looking out for you.

RICHARD I appreciate it. But I have to be here.

JOHN You're looking the MBE[17] aren't you?

RICHARD *gives* JOHN *a look.*

Rich! I thought you were a republican?[18]

RICHARD I am, I am. But... I just wouldn't mind some recognition for the work I've done over the years.

JOHN You'd have more clout over those snobs in BBC London anyway.

RICHARD Smug pricks. But who's got the PM in their studio tonight? Not them!

JOHN I wouldn't take an MBE. It's a knighthood or nothing. 'Sir John' they'll call me!

---

[17] The Most Excellent Order of the British Empire is a British order of chivalry, rewarding contributions to the arts and sciences, work with charitable and welfare organisations, and public service outside the civil service.

[18] 'Republican' in an Irish sense generally means someone who favours Irish separation from Britain. Here it refers to an Irish Unionist who simply opposes monarchy, and wants to remove the Queen as head of state.

RICHARD Richard Devlin MBE...Niamh will love it...she...would have loved it.

Beat.

JOHN She was mad for them royals, wasn't she?

RICHARD She never shut up about them.

JOHN *picks up the bust of Oliver Cromwell.*

JOHN *(dismissively)* Republicans. You won't be happy till there's some moronic president desecrating Buckinham Palace. Good looking fella, Cromwell. Handy in a civil war.

RICHARD We may see Ireland's first civil war kick off tonight.[19] Those protests outside could get nasty.

JOHN Ha! Irishmen killing each other? Like that'd ever happen.

RICHARD There's definitely a chance of trouble. It's in your hands. And God help us, with those socks and *that* tie.

JOHN What's wrong with my tie? Martha picked it. She said it's *neutral*. Is it not *neutral*?!

JOHN *rushes to check his appearance in the reflection of a mirror. He pulls out another tie from his pocket. He holds it up to his neck.*

What do you think? Red? Or blue? Blue! Red?

HANNAH *enters.*

HANNAH Rich?

RICHARD What is it?

HANNAH Grainne's here.

RICHARD Great, she's sitting in tonight.

HANNAH She's round the back at security.

---

[19] The Irish Civil War (28 June 1922 – 24 May 1923) was a conflict that followed the Irish War of Independence.

RICHARD What? I told her to queue round front like everyone else.

HANNAH She wants to speak to you.

RICHARD Now? Bloody hell, right. Bring her up, Hannah.

HANNAH I've a million other things to be doing, but fine.

HANNAH *nods and leaves.*

RICHARD Now remember, tonight's about the facts. 'Inform, educate and entertain'.[20]

JOHN I'd rather lean into 'entertain'.

RICHARD John, this referendum's stirred something up in people. The debate tonight is the last chance we'll get to contain it. So no grandstanding! The world's watching. And more importantly, the lads from SKY will be watching *you*.

JOHN *chooses the blue tie, and begins putting it on.*

JOHN Ach, nothing's signed yet. Apparently they're questioning my sex appeal... I know! That's why I need to make a bit of a splash. Give them a good sparky, sexy debate. Create the 'moment' that people will never forget.

RICHARD 'The moment'? Jesus.

JOHN Remember when I asked the Foreign Secretary about WMDs in Iraq?[21] And you were just silent...

---

[20] The phrase 'inform, educate, entertain' was coined by former Director-General of the British Broadcasting Corporation John Charles Walsham Reith to summarise the BBC's purpose. Reith is is credited with established the tradition of independent public service broadcasting in the United Kingdom, and the phrase remains part of the organisation's mission statement to this day.

[21] The Iraq War began in 2003 with the invasion of Iraq by a United States-led coalition. The Bush administration based its rationale for the war principally on the assertion that Iraq supposedly possessed weapons of mass destruction (WMDs). These WMDs were never found and the U.S. Senate later released a report that the government's pre-war statements were not supported by intelligence.

RICHARD I was.

JOHN And I know that when you're silent, that's the signal to go in for the kill! The audible wink. And we got the cunt! He admitted it. People still talk about that!

RICHARD And even more people talk about the time you picked your nose when you thought you were off-air. How many hits does that have on YouTube now?

JOHN Coming on seven million. Proving my worth as a man of the people.

JOHN *opens a locked drawer and takes out a box containing his earpiece, takes it and puts it in his pocket before returning the box to the drawer.*

RICHARD Seven figure salary?

JOHN Fingers crossed.

RICHARD Jammy bastard. And you'll be off to London I suppose?

JOHN Place to be. Here, I got you something. Look in your drawer there.

RICHARD *takes out a long wrapped object from a desk drawer. It's clearly a bottle of alcohol.*

RICHARD I wonder what this is!

RICH *unwraps in and reveals a bottle of Bushmills 16 Year old Single Malt.*

Ah John. You shouldn't have.

JOHN Celebrate our potential last show together. Shall we have a cheeky one now?

RICHARD After! I can't let you go on half-cut.

JOHN I'd give you the highest ratings we've ever had.

RICHARD And probably break up the Union.

JOHN You really think that muck-savage Keogh can convince enough boggers in the godforsaken midlands to vote for independence?

RICHARD There's a lot of boggers! And it's not just them. The right wing pricks in Belfast, the Daily Mail readers in Limerick, the stupid bastards in feckin...Longford. We need to get through this fairly and restore some bloody order.

JOHN If you want to Remain you should let me duff Keogh up a bit.

RICHARD No. It could backfire.

JOHN It'll be fun.

RICHARD Seriously now John. A debate is a very sensitive thing. One small change could make a big difference on the entire outcome of this vote. And more importantly your job prospects.

A knock at the door.

Yes?

The door opens. **HANNAH** *enters first, followed by* **GRAINNE.**

JOHN Grainne!

GRAINNE Hello.

HANNAH *receives a phonecall.*

HANNAH John, they're looking for you now. *(She answers)* Hello.

JOHN It's good to see you.

RICHARD John, please leave us alone.

HANNAH Alright, I'll call down.

JOHN I can't imagine how hard it must be for you.

RICHARD Makeup John. Now.

HANNAH The Prime Minister's almost here.

RICHARD I'll be right down.

HANNAH See you in a bit, Grainne.

> JOHN *and* HANNAH *leave.* RICHARD *closes the door behind them.*

RICHARD Sorry Grainne I don't really have any time. I'm flat out here. Did I not say to use the public entrance?

GRAINNE I don't think I can do it.

> *Pause.*

I can't sit there, with all those people. In front of all the cameras.

> *Pause.*

RICHARD I thought it would be good for you to watch the debate.

GRAINNE I can't, Dad.

RICHARD Come here.

> *They hug.*

GRAINNE I can't stop thinking about her.

> *There is a long, awkward silence. They don't know how to act around each other.*

RICHARD Did you get here, OK?

GRAINNE It was tricky. The marches have started.

RICHARD Sackville Street[22] must be a nightmare.

---

[22] Dublin's main thoroughfair was named after Lionel Sackville, 1st Duke of Dorset and Lord Lieutenant of Ireland (1750–1755). In 1924 it was renamed 'O'Connell Street' in honour of Daniel O'Connell.

GRAINNE There's like a thousand people out there. Going from Nelson's Pillar[23] to King George in Stephen's Green.[24]

RICHARD The Remainers will be out in force as well.

GRAINNE They'll probably end up meeting at College Green for a punch up.

RICHARD You didn't feel like joining them?

GRAINNE Which ones?

RICHARD Well, not the racists.

GRAINNE You can't dismiss them all like that. There's extremists on both sides.

RICHARD Oh, here we go.

GRAINNE They have legitimate grievances.

RICHARD Like what? Too many brown people?

GRAINNE Lack of representation.

RICHARD Spouting about their ancient Celtic utopia. All this nationalism, Grainne. Don't let yourself get caught up in it.

GRAINNE Is that what you told Mum? She was a nationalist.

RICHARD It's bad for the country. Did you know that Keogh is an immigrant himself?

GRAINNE I don't want to talk about politics, Dad.

RICHARD His mother is American! One of those Boston Irish trying to fund uprisings in Connacht. Half his funding is from Alopecian rednecks...

GRAINNE *What* rednecks?

---

[23] Nelson's Pillar was a large granite column capped by a statue of Horatio Nelson, built in the centre of what was then Sackville Street. It survived until March 1966, when it was severely damaged by explosives planted by Irish republicans.

[24] Stephen's Green once had a large statue of King George II at the centre of it. In May 1937 it was bombed by Irish republicans, coinciding with the coronation of King George VI.

RICHARD Alopecian. The mountains.

GRAINNE The *Appalachian* mountains, Dad. Alopecia's when your hair falls out.

RICHARD Gotcha.

They both laugh.

GRAINNE You genuinely think you're funny, don't you?

RICHARD I do, yes. *Alopecian* rednecks. That'd be some sight. Look, if you're not up for it tonight. I'll get you a car back home.

GRAINNE You're not listening.

RICHARD Well, what do you want? Do you want to watch the debate or go home?

GRAINNE Can I not stay with you?

RICHARD I can't bring you into the gallery. It's manic enough in there.

GRAINNE But you're the boss, Dad.

RICHARD Yeah, and I have responsibilities. I have to run this place.

GRAINNE Wasn't Hannah doing that when you were off?

Beat.

RICHARD Well, yes.

GRAINNE Get her to do it.

Beat.

RICHARD No, I have to do it.

GRAINNE What's the point of training Hannah if you don't let her do her job?

RICHARD I do. She ran the last show! But not tonight.

GRAINNE Dad, you don't have to do it. They've been getting on fine without you.

RICHARD Tonight is important, Grainne. It's the biggest night of the year.

GRAINNE I know, but it's only been a week.

RICHARD The Prime Minister's going to be here.

GRAINNE What am I supposed to do? I can't sit out there watching it. You haven't spoken to me in days, Dad. You argued with Mum / and she drove off...

RICHARD We didn't argue.

GRAINNE ...and died on some back road, and you're not talking to me about it and I... I don't... I just need, I need to know... I can't...

GRAINNE begins to cry and shake. RICHARD runs to her and holds her tight.

I'm sorry. I'm sorry.

RICHARD No, no, no. It's OK. I'll stay with you. We'll ummmm... We'll make it work.

GRAINNE So I can stay here?

RICHARD You can stay. I'll emmm... I'll think of something.

GRAINNE Are you sure?

RICHARD It's bring-your-daughter-to-work day. I've decided.

GRAINNE Thanks.

RICHARD Only don't tell John. His daughter's a nightmare.

GRAINNE She's a right pain in the hole!

They laugh. A knock on the door. HANNAH pops her head in.

HANNAH Richard, I don't mean to be / interrupting...

RICHARD It's no problem.

HANNAH The Prime Minister's here.

RICHARD Thanks Hannah. *(Beat)* Wait there a second.

> **RICHARD** *walks over to* **HANNAH**.

Change of plan. I want you in the gallery for tonight's show.

HANNAH Where will you be?

RICHARD I'm going to stay here. With Grainne.

HANNAH OK. OK. So I'll run the show.

RICHARD Yes.

HANNAH OK. Great. So who'll manage the floor?

RICHARD Figure it out. Hannah, I'm trusting you with this.

HANNAH Thanks Rich. Seriously. I really appreciate it.

RICHARD And Grainne won't be sitting in.

HANNAH Oh right.

RICHARD So get someone to fill her seat.

HANNAH I / don't...

RICHARD We don't want empty seats on screen.

HANNAH We don't have time to vet anyone.

RICHARD Just get someone.

> **HANNAH** *leaves*.

And tell the PM I'll be right out.

> **RICHARD** *turns to* **GRAINNE**.

Do you want to meet the Prime Minister?

GRAINNE Neo-liberal bitch.

RICHARD That's a no then. Look...sorry about the politics stuff.
I'm stressed, and / I didn't mean to be...

GRAINNE It's fine, Dad.

RICHARD Alright.

Silence.

Have you taken your tablets today?

GRAINNE Not yet.

RICHARD Do you have them with you?

GRAINNE Yes.

RICHARD Show me them.

GRAINNE *takes out a case of medication.*

Will we take them now then?

GRAINNE Dad.

RICHARD You know it puts me at ease.

GRAINNE *takes out two pills. She looks at* RICHARD, *and pops them in her mouth.*

I love you, Grainne.

GRAINNE Love you too.

RICHARD I have to go. I'll be back soon.

RICHARD *leaves, going down the stairs.*

GRAINNE *places her fingers in her mouth and pulls out the pills, unswallowed, and throws them in the bin.* RICHARD *reaches the bottom of the stairs and walks off stage.*

(o.s.) Prime Minister!

She takes out her packet of pills, looks at them, thinks for a moment, and determinedly drops them into the bin. The signal scrambles, the lights flicker. GRAINNE *is having a 'break'.*

GRAINNE *looks up. On the screen,* GRAINNE *sees* NIAMH.

GRAINNE Mum!

The lights and screen flicker.

Is that you?

GRAINNE *walks to the screen.*

The lights flicker and screen flicker, and the signal scrambles.

What happened that night?

Blackout.

Scene Two

An informational video in light-hearted animation and cartoon caricatures, with voiceover from a **REPORTER**.

REPORTER *(voice over)* This is your Guide to Irish Independence... for non-Brits. It's a long and complex story, so let's start with the basics. Where is Ireland anyway?

A map shows Ireland, unpartitioned, filled with the left part of the Union Flag.

Ireland is here. The smaller of the two islands in the British Isles[25] of the United Kingdom.

Tomorrow, the people of Ireland will go to the ballot box to see if they should become an independent country. So, how did we get here?

Way back in the olden times, Ireland was made up of many warring Kingdoms.

In 1536 Ireland was finally united, by Henry VIII of England, who (in between chopping off his wives' heads) ruled over both islands. In the Act of Union 1800, Ireland and England came together fully, forming the United Kingdom of Great Britain and Ireland.

Skip ahead a century and many in Ireland started calling for Home Rule. No, this wasn't for building regulations, but the idea of giving more power to local people. In 1912,

---

[25] In Ireland today 'The British Isles' is seen as an archaic term. 'The British and Irish Isles' or 'These Islands' are the preferred terms.

the Home Rule Act was passed,[26] and unlike the Titanic, it could not be sunk.

It created an Irish Parliament in Dublin, whilst the Imperial Parliament at Westminster ruled on the more serious matters.

It was controversial even back then! Edward Carson's Ulster Volunteers protested violently against it,[27] while Sinn Feiners thought taking over the Post Office might achieve full independence![28] However, the delicate maneuvering of the Irish First Minister John Redmond[29] made Home Rule a roaring success, leading to similar parliaments in Wales, Scotland and the English regions.[30]

So if all worked out, why the referendum?

---

[26] There were several Irish Home Rule bills put before Westminster:
The First Home Rule Bill (1886) by Gladstone (defeated in the commons)
The Second Home Rule Bill (1893) by Gladstone (passed the commons, defeated in the Lords)
The Third Home Rule Bill (1912) by Asquith (passed the commons, defeated in the Lords.)
Reintroduced 1913. (Passed the commons, defeated in the Lords.)
Reintroduced 1914. (Passed the commons, defeated in the Lords. Government then bypassed the Lords and sent the bill for Royal assent as the Government of Ireland Act 1914. It never came into force, due to the intervention of World War I (1914–18).

[27] The Ulster Volunteers was a unionist militia led by Edward Carson and James Craig, which was founded in 1912 to block Home Rule. On 28 September 1912, over 500,000 Unionists signed the Ulster Covenant, pledging to defy Home Rule by all means possible.

[28] The Easter Rising was an armed insurrection in Ireland during Easter Week, April 1916. The Rising was launched by Irish republicans to end British rule in Ireland and establish an independent Irish Republic. Members of the Irish Volunteers seized key locations in Dublin, including the General Post Office and proclaimed an Irish Republic.

[29] John Redmond was an Irish MP and leader of the Irish Parliamentary Party from 1900–1918, during the period of Asquith's Home Rule Bills.

[30] Modernly known as 'The West Lothian question', the presence of devolved parliaments within the United Kingdom raises the question of whether MPs from the devolved regions who sit in House of Commons should be able to vote on matters that affect only England, while MPs from England are unable to vote on matters that have been given to the devolved parliaments. This issue was raised around the time of the Irish Home Rule bills and several solutions were posited. One of which was devolved parliaments in all the home nations, an idea dubbed 'Home Rule All Round'.

In last year's elections, Prime Minister Ursula Lysaght's Labour party came just short of a majority. She turned to Peter Keogh's Irish Parliamentary Party[31] to form a coalition, who would only enter government under one condition: an independence referendum. The Prime Minister agreed, seeing it as unlikely to pass, but support for independence has spiked in recent months.

Those on the Leave side include Peter Keogh's IPP, the Green Party, The Scottish National Party, and several Irish boy bands, whilst on the Remain side is the Ursula Lysaght's Labour Party, The Conservatives, The Trinity College Student's Union, and Lord Bono.

Those conspicuously offering no opinion include the Queen, The Liberal Democrats and the Irish Football Association.[32]

The question is: will the people of Ireland vote tomorrow for independence? It's still too close to call.

---

[31] The Irish Parliamentary Party was formed in 1874 as the official parliamentary party for Irish nationalist Members of Parliament (MPs) elected to the House of Commons at Westminster within the United Kingdom of Great Britain and Ireland. Its central objectives were legislative independence for Ireland and land reform.

[32] The Irish Football Association is currently the governing body for the Northern Irish team, while the Republic of Ireland team are organised by the Football Association of Ireland. The IFA predates the FAI, and before Irish independence the all-island team was governed by the IFA and based in Belfast.

Scene Three

Lights up on office.

GRAINNE *is sitting on a chair, passed out and having what looks to be a mild seizure. We are seeing her 'break' from the perspective of an outsider. She's muttering under her breath and jolting. She slumps off the chair and falls behind the desk.* **HANNAH** *enters looking for her laptop.* **RICHARD**'s *desk is littered with* **JOHN**'s *unfinished bagel and coffee cup.*

HANNAH Fucking John can't clean up after himself.

GRAINNE *slowly rises from behind the table. Dazed.*

Jesus, Grainne. Scared the shite out of me.

GRAINNE Hannah? Sorry.

HANNAH What are you doing down there...you OK?

GRAINNE Yeah. I... I dropped something.

HANNAH *sees her laptop on* **RICHARD**'s *desk. She picks it up, along with the bundle of papers sitting on them.*

HANNAH Really sorry about your mum, Grainne.

GRAINNE Yeah.

HANNAH Sorry I couldn't be at the funeral.

GRAINNE Thanks for the flowers.

HANNAH She was always so nice to me.

GRAINNE She liked you.

Awkward pause. **HANNAH** *checks the time on her phone.*

HANNAH I always remember when she took us to see the Queen in Galway.

GRAINNE For someone in favour of independence, she really loved aul Lizzy.

HANNAH We had our mini flags and all.

GRAINNE Giving it socks with the waving.

HANNAH And you got lost.

GRAINNE I didn't. I ran away.

HANNAH We found you being held by the Royal bodyguards. And your mammy just barrelled past them to grab you.

GRAINNE She didn't give a fuck.

HANNAH I thought they were going to send her straight to Kilmainham,[33] but they gave us all those fridge magnets with the Queen's face on them.

GRAINNE Dad stuck them on the bin. Said it was the best place for her.

HANNAH A republican unionist and a royalist nationalist... God knows how your parents ended up together.

GRAINNE They balanced each other out.

Beat.

HANNAH I really need to go. Keogh's coming in a few minutes.

Beat.

GRAINNE Hannah, why weren't you there? At the funeral?

Beat.

HANNAH I'm sorry. I had to cover for your dad.

GRAINNE John was there.

---

[33] Kilmainham Gaol was a prison in Dublin where Irish revolutionaries, including the leaders of the 1916 Easter Rising, were imprisoned and executed. Seen principally as a site of oppression and suffering, Kilmainham Gaol was decommissioned as a prison by the Irish Free State government in 1924.

HANNAH I had to keep things running.

GRAINNE I thought you just didn't want to come.

HANNAH No, I did. I just wanted to help your dad, so he could be there for you.

GRAINNE Be there for me.

HANNAH Yeah.

GRAINNE He's barely spoken to me. No-one has.

Beat.

HANNAH Look, let's get a catch up soon. A proper one. It's been ages. But after tomorrow, yeah?

GRAINNE You're in the gallery tonight.

HANNAH Exactly, completely up to my eyes.

As HANNAH *goes to leave she collects her things from the desk and puts her hand in* JOHN's *leftover bagel, getting avocado on her hand.*

Fucking John and his avocado.

Over the next dialogue, HANNAH *is wiping her hands with a tissue.*

GRAINNE Dad obviously trusts you.

HANNAH I know. And I'm up for it. I just wish we were asking questions that actually mattered. Not this stupid referendum.

GRAINNE Why is it stupid?

HANNAH Cos people aren't actually going to vote Leave. They'd be mad.

GRAINNE I'm thinking about it.

HANNAH Are you joking?

GRAINNE Have you not considered it?

HANNAH No. The country is doing well. You work with the system you have.

GRAINNE You sound like my dad.

HANNAH doesn't reply. She finishes wiping her hands and collects the bagel and coffee cup together. She steps on the pedal of the bin to open it and drops them in. Suddenly, she notices the packet of GRAINNE's *pills in the bin.*

HANNAH What's this? Quetiapine? *(Pronounced Kwa-tia-peen.)*

GRAINNE *is silent.*

These are yours.

Silence.

GRAINNE I'm seeing Mum.

HANNAH What?

GRAINNE I'm seeing her.

Beat. HANNAH's *phone rings. She holds it for a moment, and then answers.*

HANNAH Yeah. Yeah. OK. I'll be there.

She hangs up the phone.

Keogh's here.

Beat.

Your dad told me you'd stopped your...episodes, stopped seeing things.

GRAINNE I'm getting them again.

HANNAH Since when?

GRAINNE I dunno. The last while.

HANNAH Is that why you were on the floor, have you just...?

GRAINNE Yeah.

HANNAH Fuck Grainne. Are you OK? Are you taking these?

GRAINNE No. I haven't since she died.

HANNAH Why not?

GRAINNE Because I know what I'm seeing now. I'm sure of it. Alternate realities.

HANNAH Jesus, Grainne.

GRAINNE No Hannah, listen. I'm reading this book that says what is often considered schizophrenia...

HANNAH Ah fuck sake...

GRAINNE ...could actually be the result of quantum interference between different versions of the same brain in parallel universes.

HANNAH You're fairly getting stuck into the science degree.

GRAINNE All the things I used to remember seeing or hearing... Everyone used to tell me I was crazy.

HANNAH You're not crazy...you just remember things wrong.

GRAINNE It wasn't wrong. It was different. It was what my brain experienced in parallel universes.

HANNAH Is this what they're teaching you at uni?

GRAINNE I wish! All we've done so far is circular motion and feckin magnetism. Look. Every time we make a choice, reality splits in two. Two realities that can never touch. In one reality we made one choice, in another we made a different one. And when I have my...breaks, my brain in this reality, can connect to my brain in a different reality, where different choices were made.

HANNAH Grainne, for ages you swore that you had a twin brother. You used to think the first man on the moon was a Russian.[34] And you used to call Eddy Carson's nightclub[35] on Harcourt street something weird... Coopers was it?

GRAINNE Coppers.[36]

HANNAH You pass out and when you wake up, you remember these delusions.

GRAINNE They're not delusions. They're parallel universes, alternate realities – whatever you want to call them. And it's not just one world. I've seen so many different...histories, that made me feel so lost. I didn't know who I was. I've seen hundreds... Hundreds of small hands and feet. In a septic tank.[37] Huge empty houses and frozen bodies in the street. Fire falling like rain. People turned to shadows, the skin sliding off their backs. I've seen horrible things. I took the pills because it blocked them out. But now, I see Mum.

HANNAH They're not real Grainne.

GRAINNE In a world where she's still alive.

HANNAH You're sick. You were *diagnosed.*

---

[34] The Space Race was a 20th-century competition between two Cold War rivals, the Soviet Union (USSR) and the United States (US), to achieve firsts in spaceflight capability. The USSR sent the first man into space, but it was the US which first landed a man on the moon.

[35] Sir Edward Carson was an Irish unionist politician, barrister and judge. Carson led the Ulster Volunteer Force and championed the creation of Northern Ireland. He was born at No. 4 Harcourt Street, Dublin.

[36] Copper Face Jacks Nightclub opened on Harcourt street in 1996. It was named after John Scott, 1st Earl of Clonmell, whose nickname derived from his occasional red complexion which ironically arose because of his drinking habits. Copperfaced Jack served as Lord Chief Justice of the King's Bench for Ireland from 1784 to 1789.

[37] The Bon Secours Mother and Baby Home that operated between 1925 and 1961 in the town of Tuam, County Galway, Ireland, was a maternity home for unmarried mothers and their children. In 2012, historian Catherine Corless, published an article documenting the history of the home, estimating that nearly 800 children had died there. The Home is now being investigated by a statutory commission of investigation. Excavations carried out between November 2016 and February 2017 found a significant quantity of human remains, aged from 35 foetal weeks to two to three years, interred in 'a vault with twenty chambers'. The site matched the location of a septic tank when overlaid with maps of the period of use as a workhouse.

GRAINNE I'm not schizophrenic, Hannah. Some people are, but that's not me.

HANNAH But the doctors told you.

GRAINNE Listen. That night, I went to bed and I woke up and she was lying dead on some back road. And now I'm seeing a world where she's alive.

HANNAH It was an accident Grainne.

GRAINNE No, I heard Mum and Dad arguing that night. I don't know what about.

HANNAH Have you spoken to your dad about this?

GRAINNE No, he just clams up. That's why I need to break through to her. In another world where she didn't die. To find out what their argument was about.

HANNAH (to herself) Fuck sake. (To GRAINNE – choosing her words carefully) You should talk to him.

GRAINNE He'd just force the pills on me. That's his solution to everything.

HANNAH You should try.

GRAINNE Help me Hannah.

HANNAH How?

GRAINNE Ask him what he was fighting with my mum about.

HANNAH That's not my business.

GRAINNE Why are you taking his side?

HANNAH What? There's no sides, Grainne.

GRAINNE Then help me.

HANNAH It's between you and your dad.

GRAINNE He always did like you more.

HANNAH Grainne, I'm not / getting into that.

GRAINNE Like the daughter he wanted, the one who would follow in his footsteps – now he's got you doing his job. / I bet you love that.

HANNAH I have to go. I'm not / listening to you go on like this.

GRAINNE Looking down on me, pitying me, because I haven't had a job, because I'm behind you / in life?

HANNAH Behind me?! Fuck sake, Grainne.

GRAINNE Do you know how hard it was for me to watch all of my friends go off to uni having fun when I was in hospital drugged up to my eyeballs?

HANNAH I'm not doing this for fun. I've had to work my ass off to get where I am. At least I'm trying to make a difference!

GRAINNE A difference, cleaning up after John?

HANNAH I'm not doing this again. I'm going to get Keogh. Take these.

GRAINNE I don't want them.

HANNAH's *phone rings again. She answers it. In her rush she pockets the pills.*

HANNAH *(into phone)* Yeah, yeah, I'm coming... No. No. Listen. I'll go. I'll be there...

HANNAH *hangs up her phone.*

Keogh's tweetin' that we're keeping him waiting: 'The Irish left out in the cold once again!' What a fuckin prick.

HANNAH *leaves.* GRAINNE *is left alone once more.*

Scene Four

Video report.

VOX POPS *with people on the street. They are on busy streets in Ireland, recognisable, but now with British iconography.*

REPORTER The most divisive campaign in Irish politics since the Home Rule debates of a hundred years ago. Promises aplenty. Accusations of lies. But what do the Irish people think?

VOX POP 1 *(onscreen)* We should absolutely stay.

REPORTER Why's that?

VOX POP 1 *(onscreen)* I know the types that would get elected if we were independent. A shower of slimey good-for-nothings passing 'round the brown envelopes![38] At least the English are honest about wrecking the country.

VOX POP 2 Leave! 100%! Aberdeenshire have beaten Tipp to the hurling final for the last three years. If we leave, maybe the Liam MacCarthy Cup[39] can come back to Tipp where it belongs.

REPORTER I see no reason why there won't still be an inclusive Gaelic Games –

VOX POP 2 Where it belongs!!

VOX POP 3 I think we should stay. I live in Queenstown,[40] out in Cork, and I have a sister in Liverpool. It'd be awful confusing for her wee son if he thought his auntie was in a different

---

[38] Corruption in Irish politics before the 2008 financial crash was routinely linked to politicians supposedly being bribed with 'brown envelopes' full of cash.

[39] The Liam MacCarthy Cup is given to the winner of the all-Ireland senior hurling championship. Aberdeenshire do not currently compete in the competition.

[40] Queenstown. The former English name for Cobh, County Cork.

country. He wouldn't know what was going on. We're the British Isles! How can Ireland be called a different country to the rest of the UK?

VOX POP 4 Leave. Definitely. We need to finish what O'Connell started. REPEAL! REPEAL![41]

VOX POP 5 Absolutely stay. It's very scary with these nationalists. A lot of them are really extreme. We need to make sure our rights are protected. Imagine our country ruled by those right-wing Catholic nut jobs![42] It doesn't bear thinking about!

---

[41] The Repeal Association was an Irish mass membership political movement set up by Daniel O'Connell in 1830 to campaign for a repeal of the Acts of Union of 1800 between Great Britain and Ireland.

In modern times 'Repeal' was a slogan to repeal the 8th amendment to the Irish Constitution which banned abortion.

[42] The Irish Constitution (Bunreacht na héireann) ratified in 1937, was heavily influenced by the Catholic Church.

Scene Five

In the studio, **JOHN** *sits applying makeup.* **RICHARD**
walks around him. Cameras are being set in position.
Lights are being pulled into position. **HANNAH** *checks*
the camera framing and focus on **JOHN***'s face. She also*
tests the mics (saying 'one, two, three, four' and tapping
them).

RICHARD Question... seven.

JOHN Finbar in... E seventeen. sixteen? seventeen? sixteen?

RICHARD Seventeen.

JOHN Seventeen! I know my shit, Rich.

RICHARD *covers the paper, challenging* **JOHN** *to*
remember the question.

JOHN *snaps into presenter mode.*

Pointing out that most of the great strides in social
liberalisation have come from Labour governments in
Westminster: equal marriage, women's rights, which were
passed DESPITE opposition from the Conservative Irish.[43]
How can Keogh assure him, as a young person, that an
independent Ireland will speak to his ideals?

RICHARD *nods.* **JOHN** *smirks, proud of himself.*

Keogh'll probably quote the '1916 Proclamation'[44] to answer
that. I should get a copy of it. That'd be a prop with a point.

RICHARD The Bolshevik manifesto written by a load of postmen?

---

[43] With the exception of their main policies of Land Reform and Home
Rule, the Irish Parliamentary Party often sided with the Conservative Party
in the Westminster government.
[44] See note number 29 about the 1916 easting rising. The leaders of the
rising read out a Proclamation from the steps of the GPO.

RICHARD They got off lightly for treason. They should have been shot.[45] Wasn't your man Pearson involved?

JOHN Patrick Pearson?[46] No no. He was one of the main supporters of Home Rule. Sure he was Redmond's Education Minister. Putting a paedo in charge of schools. That's the Irish Parliamentary Party for you.

RICHARD Don't be fuckin sayin that with your mic on.

JOHN Calm down. Dick...

RICHARD *looks at him disapprovingly.*

What? That's your name. Dick.

RICHARD Question nine?

JOHN Is coming from... *(He reads)* Ciara sitting in the front row, A14.

RICHARD From?

JOHN Fuckbumble-nowhere in Bogtown, County Leitrim.

RICHARD She has...

JOHN ...a debilitating health condition and wants a definitive answer on what will happen to the NHS[47] in an independent Ireland.

RICHARD She's not the only one. *(To* HANNAH*)* How are we doing?

HANNAH Four minutes.

RICHARD OK. *(To* JOHN*)* Listen, Hannah will be calling the show tonight.

---

[45] The leaders of the rising were shot for their part in it. They are often regarded as martyrs in the Irish Republican tradition.

[46] Patrick Pearse was one of the leaders of the 1916 rising, but prior to this he was one of the main supporters of the Home Rule Bill in 1912.

[47] Ireland does not have full free medical treatment at point of service. The National Health Service (NHS) in the United Kingdom is often the reason many 'small u' unionists in Northern Ireland wish to remain part of the UK.

JOHN Since when?

RICHARD Since I decided.

JOHN Whatever you say.

RICHARD Don't worry. I'll be watching. I'll have a headset... just in case.

JOHN *and* **RICHARD** *converse quietly, looking over papers, as* **HANNAH** *comes to the front and addresses the audience.*

HANNAH *(to Audience.)* Good evening everybody. Thank you all for coming out. My name is Hannah. How are we all doing? *(Beat)* I said, how are we all doing?! Great! Did you get here alright tonight? Parking's dreadful isn't it? How many of you are visiting us from out of town? Let's see some hands. Where are you from, sir? *(***HANNAH** *listens for response from a random audience member)* _____ – *(***HANNAH** *repeats the place name given to her by audience member)* _____ ah, the heart of Ireland!

We'll be ready to go in about three minutes or so. Before we do, just a few things.

Firstly, PLEASE! Remember to turn off your phones!

We'll be taking pre-designated questions only. I've already spoken to those of you who are asking questions tonight, and you should have them on cards, yes? When the time comes, can we please ask you to stand up and wait for the microphone to come to you. Then, when John – there he is over there – prompts you, please ask your questions slowly and clearly so that we all hear you.

OK, now we'll try out your applause. I will say, 'Ladies and gentlemen, please put your hands together for John Fitzgibbon', and then you will start clapping like mad. OK? Can we try that? OK.

'Ladies and gentlemen, please put your hands together for John Fitzgibbon.'

HANNAH *starts the applause and encourages the audience to partake.*

(to audience) You call that an applause?! Let's try that one more time! 'Ladies and gentlemen, please put your hands together for John Fitzgibbon.'

Applause sign. KEOGH *walks out from upstage.*

Great! Every time you see the APPLAUSE sign, give it socks! OK, we're almost ready. Talk amongst yourselves for a few minutes and we'll be good to go. Thank you.

KEOGH *approaches the audience, and waves.*

KEOGH I heard applause. I assumed it was for me.

HANNAH Mr Keogh, we're just getting the final touches ready if you could / wait back there.

KEOGH Got to feel out my battle station. Richard, terribly sorry to hear about Niamh. *(To* JOHN*)* Nice tie, John.

JOHN Well now I have to change it.

HANNAH The tie's good. Two minutes!

URSULA LYSAGHT *has come on from the side of the stage and is waving to the audience.*

PM LYSAGHT Hello, hello, yes, hello. Thank you all so much for a coming out tonight. We really appreciate it. Thank you. Thanks.

KEOGH *comes and joins her. Through the next dialogue the two of them pretend to greet each other, shake hands and then look into the audience and wave – all the while speaking through gritted teeth and muttering to each other.*

What the shit is this Peter? Coming out before the broadcast to schmooze with the audience. It'll win you no votes.

KEOGH Every little helps Ursula, when you're trying to free the country from the boot of English oppression.

PM LYSAGHT Go'way and jump in the Liffey you rabble-rousing prick.

KEOGH I'd only catch the clap from the last time you went swimming.

PM LYSAGHT Classy as always. How's your mistress?

KEOGH Young. How are your illegal donors?

PM LYSAGHT Numerous.

RICHARD Prime Minister. Mr Keogh. We'll be going live soon.

PM LYSAGHT No problem Richard. *(To the audience)* See you all soon!

KEOGH *(to audience)* Don't go easy on me now!

HANNAH Can you both please come this way for final checks? Mr Keogh – that lace is undone!

HANNAH quickly ushers them to a stage-hand who attaches radio mics to them.

KEOGH ties his shoe-lace. The following dialogue can overlap.

RICHARD They're like children.

HANNAH *(to JOHN)* One minute! Prime Minister first, then Keogh. Handshake. Up to the podiums.

JOHN Would it not be 'podia'?

HANNAH *(into headset/referring to the radio mics)* How's that? Happy?

JOHN takes his earpiece out of his pocket and into his ear.

JOHN *(into earpiece)* Hello, Elaine. How are you? ...Cheery as always! Who's mixing today?

JOHN shuffles papers. HANNAH moves the PM and KEOGH to their podia.

HANNAH So you're both standing *here*. There's water for you.

JOHN *(into earpiece)* Oh hello George. I thought you were Dave! You Ulstermen all sound the same.

HANNAH *rushes over to* RICHARD.

RICHARD Did you fill Grainne's seat?

HANNAH Just about.

RICHARD You're all good here. I'll be in my office with Grainne.

JOHN *(into earpiece)* Did anyone check that script?

RICHARD *(to* HANNAH*)* Good luck.

HANNAH Thanks Rich.

JOHN A few stray apostrophes.

RICHARD *(to* JOHN*)* Don't. Fuck. It. Up.

JOHN *gives* RICHARD *the middle finger.* RICHARD *leaves.*

HANNAH *(into earpiece)* 'Testing. John, John, can you hear me?'

JOHN *(into earpiece)* Loud and clear. *(To the politicians)* Prime Minister. Mr Keogh.

HANNAH Thirty seconds! Ready, John?

JOHN I could do with a quick poo, but I'll hold it.

HANNAH I'll be in your ear. Right, we're moving into position. Happy? Good. Standby!

(to Audience) OK everybody, let's get this show on the road. Now, do you remember what the cue is for applause?' Ladies and gentlemen...yes! Let's give it a whirl... 5, 4, 3. Ladies and gentlemen, please put your hands together for John Fitzgibbon!

APPLAUSE sign. HANNAH *runs to the gallery. We can possibly see* ELAINE *(the director) and* GEORGE *(the vision mixer).*

Scene Six

Studio. Spotlight snaps on **JOHN**. *A red TRANSMISSION
sign comes on. We see the image of him broadcast live
onto the screen.*

JOHN It's the vote that will decide Ireland's future. As the
Independence Referendum edges ever closer, welcome to
Dublin, for 'Ireland Decides'. The Prime Minister Ursula
Lysaght versus Irish First Minister Peter Keogh.

HANNAH VOICE OVER *(on headset)* Running A.

*VT of Debate Sting on main screen. Grand music, clips
of politicians, flags, etc. A drone shot zooms across the
Dublin City skyline to BBC Dublin: IRELAND DECIDES.
Lights up on full studio and gallery, where* **HANNAH** *is
calling the show. We can only hear* **HANNAH** *when she
broadcasts her voice through to* **JOHN**'s *earpiece.*

(on headset) Cue John!

JOHN Good evening agus Céad Míle Fáilte chuig BBC Baile
Átha Cliath.[48] Voting is now only one day away, in the most
important decision Ireland has ever been asked to make. And
here in BBC Dublin, hundreds of individuals divided equally
between supporters of Leave, Remain, and undecided, have
come together to listen to the final appeals from each side.
Ag labhairt i bhfábhar fágaint, seo Ceannaire of the Irish
Parliamentary Party agus Céad Aire na hÉireann Peter Keogh
agus ag labhairt i bhfábhar fanacht sa Ríocht Aontaithe,
Prime Minister Ursula Lysaght.[49] If you want to take part
at home in the debate, you can join us on social media. So
to kick us off, opening arguments. Mr Keogh.

---

[48] 'And a hundred thousand welcomes to BBC Dublin'.
[49] 'Speaking in favour of leaving, the leader of the Irish Parliamentary Party
and First Irish Minister Peter Keogh speaking in favour of staying in the
UK, Prime Minister Ursula Lysaght.'

HANNAH VOICE OVER You were supposed to put the PM first in your spiel John.

KEOGH Prime Minister, a dhaoine uaisle agus gach duine sa bhaile[50]...this is an extraordinary time for us all. The eyes of the world are focused on Ireland as we look to complete the Home Rule journey we started over a hundred years ago. The Irish Parliament has done so much work in that time, but there is still much, far too much, that is controlled at Westminster. We can't stop illegal wars. We can't stop the poor and disabled bearing the brunt of welfare cuts. We can't set our own tax rates to attract global business. Now we can change all of that. We can take back control[51] over our laws, our taxes, our borders, and security. The Empire, they say, the so-called 'United' Kingdom...it's crap, but we have no alternative. I'm afraid we do have an alternative. And it's a glorious alternative. Putting Ireland's future in Ireland's hands. You know, sometimes voting doesn't make much difference. Tomorrow, it really does. Tóg smacht ar chinnúint na héireann agus votáil Leave.[55]

APPLAUSE sign.

JOHN Go raibh míle maith agat First Minister.[52.5] And now to open the debate for the Remain side, Prime Minister Ursula Lysaght.

PM LYSAGHT Tráthnóna Mhaith daoibh go léir.[53] It's great to be back in Dublin. I grew up here. And as a proud Dubliner, I feel privileged to be the Prime Minister of our great Family of Nations. This is the choice of a lifetime. It goes to the heart of the kind of country we want to be. Think of your children. We don't want to cut them off from opportunity.

---

[50] 'ladies and gentlemen, and everyone at home'
[51] 'Take back control' was a prominent slogan used by the Vote Leave campaign in the run up to the UK's in/out referendum on EU membership in 2016.
[55] 'Take control of Ireland's destiny and vote leave'
[52.5] 'Thank you First Minister'
[53] 'Good evening to you all'

Throughout this evening, Peter Keogh is going to try and sell you a vision of Irishness. An insular, exclusionary, backward-looking vision. I do not subscribe to that. The greatest Irishmen and women have always been those who looked outward to the world. And we have to be proud of that tradition. Even Saint Patrick himself, our patron saint, was a Welshman.[54] I ask you to not forget that Britishness is in our history. It's in the stories of our heroes. It's in our blood. That's why we should vote Remain.

APPLAUSE sign.

HANNAH VOICE OVER Let's go John. Onto the questions.

The microphone is brought to **QUESTIONER 1.**

JOHN Thank you Prime Minister. Anois mar go bhfuil cloiste againn ón dá thaobh...[55] Let's go to our first question, I believe from a Leave supporter. What's your name and where are you from?

QUESTIONER 1 I'm _____ from _____. I've heard that we might have to start using euros in an independent Ireland. I'll be retiring soon, and my pension is in pounds. Will that be safe if we Leave?

JOHN Retiring? What is your skin care regime? First Minister Keogh.

KEOGH Go raibh míle maith agat as ucht an cheist sin[56] _____. I love sterling. When we move forward, there's no reason why we can't keep using sterling.

JOHN Short and sweet. Prime Minister?

PM LYSAGHT You're right to be worried _____. Staying in the UK is the only way to maintain control of our currency. If

---

[54] Saint Patrick was born in Roman Britain. His birthplace is not known with any certainty; various claims place it in England, Scotland or Wales.
[55] 'Now that we have heard from both sides'
[56] 'Thank you for that question'

we left, it would be unlikely that Ireland would be able to keep the pound.

KEOGH Well now, Ecuador, for example, uses the US dollar; we could keep using sterling if we wanted to, Prime Minister.[57]

PM LYSAGHT I have a lot of respect for the people of Ecuador, but their main export is bananas.[58] How many banana trees do you see growing along the Shannon? Staying in the UK is the only way to have influence and control over the pound. If we left, we'd have to have a whole new currency or more likely, we'd switch to euros[59] and be controlled by Brussels.

KEOGH And if we decided we wanted to move to the euro, or establish a whole new currency, well that would be a decision for the people, wouldn't it?

HANNAH Wrap this up John.

JOHN I think we'll hold that there, before we slip up on any banana skins. We've quite a lot to get through tonight. Can we get the next question please?

QUESTIONER 2 Hello. I'm _____ from _____. You spoke of Europe there. My daughter is currently living in Spain. Something she can only do because of the EU. Would Ireland still be in the EU if we do this thing?

HANNAH The Prime Minister.

JOHN Céad Aire Keogh.

KEOGH Thank you _____. The answer is: absolutely. You'd have to be mad to want to leave the EU! Not one country has ever seriously suggested leaving *that* union. You know, we're not *complete* fools! The EU was a great help in reuniting

---

[57] When Ireland gained its independence in 1922, Ireland had its own currency, The Irish Pound, but it was pegged to the British Pound until 1978, when an exchange rate was introduced due to Ireland joining the European Monetary System.
[58] Equador exports US$3.2 billion of bananas a year (23.7% of total banana exports). However Irish company Fyffes is one of the largest banana companies in the world. Accounting for 6% of bananas sold worldwide.
[59] Ireland joined the eurozone on 1st January 1999.

East and West Berlin, and I'm sure they'll be just as great in separating 'East' and 'West Britain'.

JOHN Prime Minister.

PM LYSAGHT I agree with Peter. Certainly no-one has any appetite for that.[60] We're stronger together, safer together, and more prosperous together. And I'm using Peter's exact argument as to why we should Remain in the UK. An Ireland within the UK is much like a UK within the EU – stronger, safer and more prosperous. And I believe we agreed to take turns answering questions first, John.

JOHN You can have the next two Prime Minister.

HANNAH VOICE OVER *(into earpiece)* Alternate between them, John!

Lights snap down on studio and gallery (including video) and up on office. **RICHARD** *is looking out at the debate speaking into his headset.* **HANNAH** *is still talking to* **JOHN** *on her headset, but we cannot hear her. We are just in the office with* **RICHARD** *and* **GRAINNE,** *the debate continues below them, but the lights are down and the audience cannot see what is happening.* **GRAINNE** *sits on the desk. Her bag is next to her. She is reading a copy of 'Parallel Universes: The Search for Other Worlds' by Fred Alan Wolf. A copy of 'The Subtle Knife' by Philip Pullman sits half fallen out of her bag.*

RICHARD Ah fuck sake, John's already trying to rile them up!

RICHARD *moves to grab his headset pack, but stops himself.*

(to himself) No, no, let her be. She's got it. *(To* **GRAINNE***)* You OK, there Grainne?

GRAINNE Yeah. Were they alright with me being here?

---

[60] Support for the EU is generally between 70% and 90% in Ireland.

RICHARD Of course. Twitter's kicking off... 'Fitzgibbon's tie'is trending.

RICHARD *looks back into the room and sees* **GRAINNE** *reading her book.*

You not watching?

GRAINNE *looks at him.*

You must be the only one. At least twelve million people tuned in. One of the biggest nights in Irish history.

Beat.

Is that for uni?

GRAINNE Kinda.

RICHARD Good. What is it?

GRAINNE It's a physics book.

RICHARD Speculation. It's all speculation. *(To* **GRAINNE***)* What's it about?

GRAINNE Physics.

RICHARD Hannah's not doing too badly here. She'll be Director General before she's forty.

GRAINNE I'd say she wouldn't mind that.

Beat as **RICHARD** *watches the debate.*

Dad.

RICHARD Yeah?

GRAINNE Can we talk about Mum?

RICHARD What about her?

GRAINNE How was she before she died?

RICHARD *(to* **GRAINNE***)* I'm sorry. I know we haven't talked properly, Grainne.

GRAINNE Well you've been / pretty busy...

RICHARD Give the PM a chance to finish, for fuck sake. *(To* GRAINNE*)* What was that?

GRAINNE You've been busy.

RICHARD We should make time.

GRAINNE When?

RICHARD After this is over. I promise. We'll go and we'll talk properly. Go to Bewley's. Get that hot chocolate your mum loved?

GRAINNE No cream.

RICHARD No cream. Or maybe spend a few days away? Get the train to Londonderry,[61] see your cousins?

GRAINNE Dad, you're acting like things are normal.

RICHARD We can't wallow.

GRAINNE It's been less than a week, Dad.

RICHARD Keogh's sharp as a whip tonight.

GRAINNE I remember having dinner that night. Ye weren't really talking. I went to my room and I could hear you arguing.

RICHARD We weren't arguing.

GRAINNE I heard you.

RICHARD Grainne, I'm glad you're here tonight. I am. But I have to watch this.

Lights snap down on office and up on studio and gallery (including video).

HANNAH OK, next question, the public sector.

---

[61] The names of the city of Derry or Londonderry in Northern Ireland are the subject of a naming dispute between Irish nationalists and unionists. Generally nationalists favour using the name Derry, and unionists Londonderry. There is no direct train between Dublin and Derry/ Londonderry

JOHN An chéad cheist eile.[62] Please state your name and where you're from and then read your question.

QUESTIONER 3 Hello, my name is _____ from _____, I work for the civil service. The percentage of people who are employed in the public sector in Ireland is higher than in the other regions of the UK, at over 32%. How would this work in an independent Ireland? Could we afford it?[63]

JOHN Oooh. A civil servant in our midst. Don't audit me! Prime Minister.

PM LYSAGHT Thank you John. I come from a long line of Labour politicians who care deeply about this island. This stretches as far back as the UK's first Labour Prime Minister, James Connolly[64] – a Scotsman, who actually lived in Belfast for a time. And as a Labour politician, this is what scares me about Mr Keogh. High public sector employment is a good thing. That's millions of people with good jobs and good pensions doing good work for the people of Ireland. If we left this great Union, no we could not afford it.

JOHN And Mr Keogh.

KEOGH The question is not 'could we afford it?'. It's 'could we afford not to?'.

PM LYSAGHT I think the question was very clearly 'could we afford it?', Peter.

HANNAH Reiterate the question, John.

JOHN Very funny Prime Minister, but Mr Keogh let *you* speak. Let's give him the same courtesy.

PM LYSAGHT Certainly.

---

[62] 'The next question.'

[63] Northern Ireland has very high public sector employment. Much higher than the Republic of Ireland. This disparity is often quoted in arguments against the unification of Ireland.

[64] James Connolly was a Scottish-born Irish republican and socialist leader. He was executed by a British firing squad because of his leadership role in the Easter Rising. He did indeed live in Belfast for a time.

KEOGH Thank you. It's 'could we afford not to?' The reason that public sector employment is so high in Ireland is that we are a rump state. We cannot set our own tax rates to attract business. In the devolved Dublin Parliament, my party has worked tirelessly to counter British economic centralisation. Our 'Rural Works' programme has seen jobs go up in the countryside, with people returning to their hometowns to live, to raise families. If we leave the UK, we will see the towns and villages of Ireland rejuvenated!

HANNAH What stats does he have on that?

JOHN Does an extra Tesco in Moneygall make it an industrial powerhouse?

KEOGH At least we are trying. If we were independent, we would have a more competitive corporation tax to attract business. More business, more jobs.

JOHN He has a point. Prime Minister?

PM LYSAGHT When Keogh talks about tax rates, what he really means is right-wing economic policies, which will damage safety nets such as social housing, the NHS, and pensions. *These* are the things Mr Keogh will gut in order to put money into the pockets of Google, Amazon and Facebook.[65] Not to mention that the uncertainty of an independent Ireland would threaten recession.

KEOGH Níl sé sin fíor![66]

PM LYSAGHT That would not rejuvenate the towns and villages of Ireland, but decimate them!

KEOGH Not true.

PM LYSAGHT We can not afford an independent Ireland!

---

[65] Ireland has a reputation for allowing large multinational corporations to be based there without paying a lot of tax. Many technology companies such as Google and Facebook have their european headquarters in Dublin.
[66] 'Simply not true!'

KEOGH Cailleach an uafáis![67]

PM LYSAGHT It would be economic suicide. Independence is a lose-lose game for everybody. United we stand, divided we fall. We cannot leave our brothers and sisters across the Irish sea, who need us as much as we need them.

KEOGH Scare-mongering!

PM LYSAGHT We Brits must stick together.

KEOGH Maybe you should stay over there then.

PM LYSAGHT I beg your pardon?

Lights down on studio (including video off), lights up on office.

RICHARD He didn't just say that did he? That's a slam dunk for Lysaght! Fucking Home Run!

GRAINNE What happened that night?

RICHARD *(to GRAINNE)* What do you mean?

GRAINNE After I went to sleep. Like, specifically. What did you argue about?

RICHARD Grainne. I know how you're feeling. You're feeling guilty.

GRAINNE Why would I feel guilty?

RICHARD *turns to her.*

RICHARD It was just a normal night. We had dinner with you. You went on to bed. I think we watched some telly and then, she said she was heading out... *(To himself)* Wait, that couldn't be right... Did that person say 32%?

RICHARD *starts to scroll through his Ipad, looking for the stats.*

GRAINNE And then?

---

[67] 'Scare-mongering!'

RICHARD ...and then, I got the call from the police.

GRAINNE But it just doesn't make sense Dad. Like, where was she going?

RICHARD She was always going for drives...it was an accident, love.

GRAINNE Was it an accident?

RICHARD Grainne, the police were very thorough. There were no other cars on the road. Let's just get through this debate, alright?

GRAINNE Dad?

RICHARD Believe me Grainne, if there was anyone to blame – some drunk driver – some idiot on his phone – I'd have found out where they lived and I'd've – *(To himself)* I'm sure that's not right.

GRAINNE Maybe she meant it?

RICHARD *(to* GRAINNE*)* Meant what?

GRAINNE Maybe she...you know, wanted to do it.

RICHARD No. No. Grainne put that out of your head right now.

GRAINNE But that could be it!

RICHARD It isn't. I know that for a fact.

GRAINNE How?

RICHARD Because...the police told me, there were no other cars on the road, no foul play. She had tried to stop...it was just...another accident on Irish roads. *(To himself)* There it is, I knew thirty two was too high.

GRAINNE Maybe she changed her mind at the last moment.

RICHARD Stop that talk right now! Right, fuck.

RICH *takes out a set of cans and turns them on.*

(into earpiece) Fitzy, you blue-tie bastard. Ireland's at 27% public employment, not thirty two.

Lights down on office and up on studio and gallery (including video). **JOHN** *is confused to hear* **RICHARD**'s *voice. We hear* **RICH**'s *voice as a voice over.*

HANNAH Rich? What's going on?

JOHN Em...

RICHARD Say it, twenty seven, not thirty two.

HANNAH Rich! I've got this!

JOHN I'm just getting word from our fact-checkers that Irish employment in the public sector is 27%, not 32% as claimed.

KEOGH But the point still stands. It's still a lot higher than British regions and neighbouring countries, and it's a drain on our economy.

PM LYSAGHT When this fact is brought up, you care about the economy. But when we talk about the economic implications of breaking away from the 4th largest economy in the world,[68] suddenly then it's about sovereignty.

KEOGH It *is* about sovereignty. Sovereignty and the ability for the Irish people to steer their own destiny. I'm explaining how we will do that.

PM LYSAGHT The people of Ireland know your tricks Peter. Empty rhetoric. You do not represent the majority of opinion!

RICHARD Bring up the poll, John.

HANNAH You corrected the mistake Rich, now butt out.

JOHN *holds up the poll.*

JOHN Excuse me Prime Minister, but we have here an Ipsos-MORI poll, which suggests the contrary – that Leave are indeed ahead.

RICHARD Prop. Point.

---

[68] The United Kingdom is currently the 5th largest economy in the world.

PM LYSAGHT And the other polls show the majority are in favour of Remain. We can't rely on polls. What matters is how people vote tomorrow.

HANNAH Rich, get out of his ear. Am I running this or you?

Lights snap down on studio (including video off) and up on office.

RICHARD You are! I'm just here to help.

GRAINNE Why did she leave?

RICHARD Grainne, I'm trying to...

GRAINNE Were you fighting?

RICHARD We were talking.

GRAINNE Did you make her leave?

RICHARD *(into earpiece)* Keep them on their toes John.

GRAINNE Dad! Would you listen to me?

RICHARD *(into earpiece)* You can cut her off now.

HANNAH Fuck sake.

GRAINNE Stop talking to John and fucking talk to me!

RICHARD Grainne, would you be quiet for two seconds?

GRAINNE No. There's a reason she got into that car. There's a reason she died.

RICHARD That's how you do it John!

GRAINNE I need to know what it was.

RICHARD What reason? There's no reason.

GRAINNE In another reality, she survived. So, something happened which caused her death.

RICHARD Another reality? Grainne...

RICHARD takes off his headset and gives GRAINNE his full attention.

Grainne, you've had another episode?

Beat. GRAINNE *stares him down.*

I should have thought, Grainne. With the stress...it's obviously made it worse. I'm sorry.

GRAINNE I'm not sick.

RICHARD Let's get you to the doctors tomorrow /and we can...

GRAINNE What? Up my dose? I don't need to up the / dose of my fuckin medication.

RICHARD Yes, if that's / what you need.

GRAINNE You're always jumping to those fucking pills as if it's some easy fix that'll make everything all better. Well they won't make this better. They won't bring her back!

RICHARD Neither will refusing to deal with your illness! You know that would upset her!

GRAINNE At least I'm thinking about her!

RICHARD It's not real Grainne!

GRAINNE It is. I can see other realities.

RICHARD No you can't! Your mother wanted you to live in *this* world! Why won't you do that?

GRAINNE Why won't you answer my questions?

RICHARD It was an accident.

GRAINNE If it was an accident then what are you hiding?

Lights down on office and up on studio and gallery (including video).

HANNAH OK. John. Next question – post codes.

JOHN *looks directly into the camera. He's not impressed.*

JOHN Now for some real hard-hitting stuff. Post codes!

PATRICK, *a man in the audience stands up and speaks up at the studio floor.*

PATRICK I'd like to ask a question.

JOHN *is confused. The man isn't on the list.*

JOHN Who said that?

PATRICK I did.

HANNAH VOICE OVER He's not on the list.

PATRICK The Prime Minister is asking us to Remain, but can she not see that we aren't an equal partner in this Union?

JOHN Where's that question coming from?

KEOGH An excellent point young man!

HANNAH Tell him no, John!

PATRICK How can she stand leading a country that's abused her own people?

JOHN Well, that's quite the question...

PM LYSAGHT Can we move on?

HANNAH Move on, John.

KEOGH Someone's finally talking sense.

HANNAH Designated questions only!

Beat. **JOHN** *listens in for Rich.*

JOHN Yes, young man. Can we get him a microphone please?

HANNAH What are you doing?!

The microphone is brought to **PATRICK**.

PM LYSAGHT *(quietly)* John?

HANNAH John, we don't know what he's going to say!

JOHN *(under his breath)* Exactly. *(Aloud)* Young man, please state your name and where you're from.

PATRICK *(calmly)* I'm Patrick, from Belfast.

Beat.

JOHN And could you reiterate your question to the Prime Minister please, Patrick?

PATRICK Yes. I want to know how the Prime Minister can stand leading a country that's abused her own people?

PM LYSAGHT *(quietly)* Abused?

HANNAH John.

JOHN You seem like a passionate young man Patrick...with an interesting question... Prime Minister, have you an answer?

HANNAH Back to the fucking post codes!

PM LYSAGHT Em, Patrick, isn't it? I understand your point. In the long history of our nations, there have been *mistakes*. But that's where it remains. In history.

JOHN Mr Keogh. Do you have anything to add?

KEOGH Yes I do. A Phadraig. You're right. The British Government has failed us. In many ways, we're a glorified colony.

PM LYSAGHT Excuse me Peter. The government contains many Irish officials who care deeply about the welfare of the Irish people. Myself included.

HANNAH Onto the next questions.

KEOGH They've failed us. And not just us.

JOHN Who else have they failed Mr Keogh?

KEOGH They've failed Scotland. They've failed Wales. They've failed the working classes of England. They've failed everyone outside London's M25! The British Government always has and always will care only about the wellbeing of the London stock markets and the jewels in the crown. Nothing else!

HANNAH John!

PATRICK What about the penal laws?[69]

PM LYSAGHT The what?

PATRICK Do you not remember those?

PM LYSAGHT Of course I do.

PATRICK What about the famine genocides?[70] What about the destruction of our language, our ancient codes, our culture? The Final Solution of Ireland, was it?

HANNAH This guy's a wacko.

PM LYSAGHT John, what is this?

HANNAH Next question!

KEOGH The young man has a point.

JOHN What is the official government position on the Famine Prime Minister?

PM LYSAGHT What?

KEOGH Come on Prime Minister. We're all waiting.

PM LYSAGHT You have to understand what we can achieve is enhanced by being at the table where the decisions are made!

KEOGH Padraig has raised an important issue. What is the problem with ending colonial presence on this island once and for all?

PATRICK What about the murder of Irish children in workhouses?

HANNAH End this!

---

[69] The Penal Laws were a series of draconian laws imposed in an attempt to force Irish Catholics and Protestant dissenters to accept the established Church of Ireland. They included bans on voting, holding public office, and strict laws on land ownership.

[70] The Great Famine was a period of mass starvation and disease in Ireland from 1845 to 1849. About one million people died and more than a million emigrated, causing the island's population to fall by between 20% and 25%. It was caused by a potato blight and exacerbated by the British government's economic policy of laissez-faire capitalism.

PATRICK What about the evictions of our great grandfathers from the homes that they built?

PM LYSAGHT John—

HANNAH Fucking end this!

PATRICK What about the corpses left in ditches for the rats to fester or the dogs to gorge on?

JOHN You have a great deal of anger, am I right?

PATRICK What about the women, maddened by hunger, driven to eat the flesh of their own dead daughters?!

JOHN This referendum has certainly stirred some tempers.

PATRICK What about people leaving from every port in Ireland, to die on coffin ships or live destitute wandering the streets of Northern England?!

JOHN That was in the past. / Now if you'd...

PATRICK It was one hundred and seventy four years ago.

KEOGH Under British rule!

JOHN Now listen / you can't...

PATRICK One million dead!

PM LYSAGHT We have to move on.

PATRICK We can't move on.

PM LYSAGHT It was a long time ago.

PATRICK *(to the audience)* It was YESTERDAY! Even though it's not taught in schools, and we've all forgotten. I still feel the trauma. We all do. And we always will! *(To PM LYSAGHT)* Can't you understand that?!

PM LYSAGHT Of course I do!

PATRICK No you don't! You don't understand at all! As long as you get your votes, you don't give a fuck how I feel, how we feel. To you, we're just the shit on your shoe.

Lights up on office. Both office and studio are fully lit.

RICHARD Grainne I'm not— Wait. What? What the fuck is going on down there?! Jesus Christ. *(Into earpiece)* JOHN!

JOHN Young man. I understand you're angry, but I can't have you speaking to the Prime Minister like that anymore. We will need to move on to another question...

PATRICK What? It's the truth!

JOHN I'm sorry. We need a rational debate, not a shouting match.

PATRICK *(violently)* Don't try to silence me you prostitute pressman! You're the hired liars of the enemy!

JOHN Now, I'm sorry / you feel that way but—

RICHARD Hannah – what is this?

HANNAH I'm trying! John's not listening!

PATRICK *(violently)* You're the bitches of the oppressor!

RICHARD Shut it the fuck down, John! Fuck this, I'm going down there.

GRAINNE No Dad, don't...

RICHARD *runs down the stairs and stands at the edge of the studio floor.* GRAINNE *stays in the office.*

PM LYSAGHT Young man, as British citizens / we have to –

PATRICK I am not a citizen of the British state. I am a subject of the British Empire! And I cannot trust a government that did that to us!

KEOGH You're right. It's unforgivable!

PATRICK And who was there to take over the land left vacant? Foreigners!

KEOGH Ah well –

PATRICK Millions of people from all over the globe who have poured into this country under the banner of Empire.

JOHN Patrick we will not have / that talk.

PATRICK These Jews! Muslims! And blacks! Who are as different to us as we are to the Brits!

PM LYSAGHT Get this racist Leave voter off air!

RICHARD *(into earpiece)* Tee up the adverts!

HANNAH They're ready.

KEOGH All my supporters are not racists, Ursula.

PATRICK Rape gangs! Who cover their faces! And don't even try to integrate with society!

PM LYSAGHT Not all Leave voters are racist.

RICHARD Get him out of here!

PM LYSAGHT But certainly all racists are Leave voters.

JOHN Could you repeat that Prime Minister?

PM LYSAGHT Well no, what I meant was –

PATRICK We've been invaded for too long. First by the Brits and now by *vermin*!

The lights flicker.

GRAINNE Dad, I see her! Mum! Mum!

GRAINNE *begins having a break, the large screen starts flickering.*

KEOGH And now we see her true feelings!

PATRICK Everything good in Ireland has been achieved by the Irish, and the Irish alone.

PM LYSAGHT It's his feelings you should be worried about!

RICHARD GET HIM OUT NOW!

The lights flicker. The screen briefly shows NIAMH distressed. GRAINNE has a seizure.

GRAINNE Mum!

PATRICK BREHON LAW NOT SHARIA LAW!![71] BREHON LAW NOT SHARIA LAW!! BREHON LAW NOT SHARIA LAW!!

JOHN Security!

HANNAH They're on their way.

PM LYSAGHT One of your supporters Mr Keogh!

RICHARD Someone shut him down!

KEOGH He does not represent my views.

GRAINNE Dad, I see her! Mum! Mum!

> **PM LYSAGHT** *and* **KEOGH** *continue to argue.* **RICHARD** *signals to ushers to shut* **PATRICK** *down. The image of* **NIAMH** *flickers.* **PATRICK** *runs out of the theatre shouting:*

PATRICK BREHON LAW NOT SHARIA LAW!! BREHON LAW NOT SHARIA LAW!! BREHON LAW NOT SHARIA LAW!!

RICHARD *(into earpiece)* Cut to adverts.

> *The image of* **NIAMH** *becomes clear.*

GRAINNE Mum!

HANNAH CUTTING TO ADVERTS!

NIAMH *(on screen)* She goes or I go!

> *Blackout. Interval.*

---

[71] Brehon law comprised the statutes which governed everyday life in Early Medieval Ireland. Sharia law is a religious law forming part of the Islamic tradition.

ACT TWO

Scene One

A Vote Remain advert plays on the screens praising the great Irishmen and women who shaped the Empire.

PRESENTER *(voice over)* In the two hundred years since the Act of Union, we Irish have defined British culture. Wilde, Swift and Shaw dominated the London theatre scene, while a farmer from Monaghan[72] became the UK's poet laureate. Today, Irish actors play those quintessentially British roles of James Bond and Dr Who[73] and the great bastion of British Culture, The Abbey Theatre,[74] is lauded as one of the best Receiving Houses in the world, bringing works from all over the Empire.

Image of The Abbey Theatre with a Union Jack fluttering overhead.

---

[72] Patrick Kavanagh (1904–1967) was an Irish poet and novelist born on a farm in Co. Monaghan. His best-known works include the novel Tarry Flynn, and the poems 'On Raglan Road' and 'The Great Hunger'.
[73] Pierce Brosnan is an Irish actor who has portrayed James Bond. No Irish actors have portrayed Dr Who, although Paul McGann has Irish heritage.
[74] The Abbey Theatre, also known as the National Theatre of Ireland, is one of the country's leading cultural institutions. First opening to the public on 27 December 1904, the Abbey was the first state-subsidised theatre in the English-speaking world. In its early years, the theatre was closely associated with the writers of the Irish Literary Revival.

Due to the tireless efforts of Douglas Hyde[75] and the Gaelic League, Irish sports quickly spread throughout the rest of the Empire. This year, Canada won their first ever Gaelic Football World Cup, breaking three years of South African dominance in the sport.

Image of Croke Park, with a Canadian player lifting a cup similar to the Sam Maguire.

The UK's only ever Olympic medal for painting came from that great British painter, Jack B. Yeats, with his famous painting *The Liffey Swim*.[76]

Image of Yeat's 'The Liffey Swim', which now has Union Jacks flying from the lamp posts.

And in the 2012 Olympics, over a third of all Team UK medals came from Irish athletes.

Image of an Irish boxer, Katie Taylor,[77] wrapped in the Union Jack, getting a medal.

The Irish have always been great fighters! At home, the Irish were leaders in the war effort, and in in the military, some of the top British minds have hailed from the Emerald

---

[75] Douglas Hyde helped found Conradh na Gaeilge (the Gaelic League) to encourage the preservation of Irish culture, music, dance and language. A new generation of Irish republicans (including Pádraig Pearse, Éamon de Valera, Michael Collins and Ernest Blythe), became politicised through their involvement in Conradh na Gaeilge. Uncomfortable at the growing politicisation of the movement, Hyde resigned the presidency in 1915.

[76] The first Olympic medal won by the Irish Free State was a silver medal in 1924, awarded to Jack Butler Yeats for his 1923 painting *The Liffey Swim*. Painting ceased to be a category of the Olympics after the 1948 games. Since 1952 a non-competitive art and cultural festival has been associated with each Games.

[77] Katie Taylor was the flag bearer for Ireland at the 2012 London Olympics opening ceremony before going on to win an Olympic gold medal in the lightweight division. Taylor turned professional in 2016.

Isle. From the Duke of Wellington,[78] to John Redmond's Irish Volunteers, right up to that decorated World War Two General Michael Collins,[79] whose pioneering guerrilla warfare tactics deep in German territory are credited with shortening the war by years.

So don't forget those great men and women who have gone before us.

Great Irishmen, yes. Great Britons also.

Don't Cut Yourself Off. Vote Remain.

End on a pint of Guinness, which has a Crown[80] embossed on the glass, instead of a Harp.

Cut to:

A news report.

REPORTER Trouble is stirring in Dublin as the peaceful march to express support for the Remain campaign has become embroiled in a clash with Leave protestors in the area around Kildare Street. Two people have been arrested. The numbers of protestors is growing on both sides and the police are currently trying to keep the peace. Meanwhile, the 'Ireland Decides' debate at BBC Dublin has been temporarily paused due to an interruption. Reports are that one of the questioners turned violent after a racist tirade.

---

[78] The Duke of Wellington was one of the leading military and political figures of 19th-century Britain, serving twice as Prime Minister, and defeating Napoleon at the Battle of Waterloo in 1815. He was born into an Anglo-Irish aristocratic family in Ireland, but did not consider himself Irish, seeing the country as a 'nation of scoundrels'. Daniel O'Connell famously said of the Duke of Wellington, "to be sure he was born in Ireland, but being born in a stable does not make a man a horse."

[79] Michael Collins was an Irish revolutionary, soldier and politician. He was a leading figure in the early-20th-century Irish struggle for independence, gaining fame as a guerrilla warfare strategist. He planned many successful attacks on British forces, such as the assassination of key British intelligence agents in November 1920. He was shot and killed in an ambush by anti-Treaty forces on 22 August 1922.

[80] The emblem for Guinness is a Harp.

Footage of **PATRICK** *(face blurred) being escorted down a corridor by stewards, and pushing the camera out of his face.*

Scene Two

Lights up. Studio. **JOHN** *is standing by the edge of the studio floor.* **RICHARD** *paces. The* **PM** *and* **KEOGH** *are both frantically speaking into their phones.*

JOHN I thought I handled it very well.

RICHARD You didn't do a bloody thing.

JOHN It was cracking TV! Did you hear what the PM said?

RICHARD It was a shambles.

JOHN I did what you wanted.

RICHARD I wanted it?!

JOHN You did an Iraq!

RICHARD What?

JOHN You gave me the wink.

RICHARD Winks don't make noises, John!

HANNAH *comes over.*

HANNAH Why didn't you listen to me, John?!

RICHARD If I don't respond, then continue as normal.

HANNAH I told you he wasn't approved.

PM LYSAGHT *(on phone)* OK. OK. OK.

RICHARD How long do we have?

HANNAH We can stall for another seven minutes, but then we're back on.

RICHARD This isn't happening.

HANNAH We can't run campaign ads all night.

The **PM** *darts over.* **KEOGH** *is still on his phone.*

PM LYSAGHT Good. Do it. *(She hangs up her phone)* What the fuck was that?

JOHN We have everything under –

PM LYSAGHT I thought this was the BBC!

RICHARD Prime Minister, we apologise.

PM LYSAGHT Who let that bastard in!??!

RICHARD It was an unfortunate /oversight.

PM LYSAGHT Was he vetted?

JOHN Prime Minister, we have to remember –

PM LYSAGHT Let the big boys speak, you sack of melted ice-cream. Richard – what happened?

RICHARD Apologies, Prime Minister. There was a last minute seat change and it seems our producer Hannah wasn't as thorough as she should have been.

HANNAH *is visibly annoyed.*

HANNAH What?

RICHARD It should have been from a pre-approved list, but she seems to have picked a random person off the street.

HANNAH I'm sorry Prime Minister but –

PM LYSAGHT *(ignoring* **HANNAH***)* It should have been shut down immediately.

RICHARD Yes Prime Minister.

PM LYSAGHT It's a security risk for one thing. Inciting violence!

RICHARD I know.

PM LYSAGHT Why did you give him a platform?

RICHARD That's all on John.

JOHN Excuse me?

RICHARD John we all saw it.

JOHN I was simply / doing my job.

RICHARD Please we're trying to / keep things together here –

JOHN The absolute cheek of you, you used condom.

RICHARD I'll jam my foot so far up your arse –

JOHN Go on then!

JOHN taunts RICHARD by presenting his bottom.

PM LYSAGHT Stop with the handbags! As far as I'm concerned, you're all to blame. Get a handle on this! No more surprises. And no more questions that haven't been vetted by my team.

RICHARD With respect Prime Minister, I need to retain editorial control.

PM LYSAGHT You will not retain control if you can't control it! You lock this thing down...or I'm walking.

RICHARD Prime Minister, do you really want to end the debate on that note – calling all Leave supporters racist?

PM LYSAGHT Fine. But if there's ANY more funny business, you can say goodbye to this studio. And your chance of an MBE.

Beat.

(beat) Only the questions pre-approved by my team, and read out by John. OK? Can you handle that?

RICHARD Yes Prime Minister.

The PM walks offstage. KEOGH wanders over.

KEOGH Tricky business getting these things balanced.

RICHARD Yes Mr Keogh. We apologise for the interruption. We should have things up and running again soon.

KEOGH No need to apologise. It's good to listen to everyone. It was good to hear Ursula's *true* feelings. You're doing a great job.

KEOGH *smiles and walks off.*

RICHARD Fuck!

JOHN What the fuck was that?

RICHARD She's got us by the balls now.

JOHN 'Oh Prime Minister, it was all John's fault. I'm so sorry Prime Minister'.

RICHARD Don't you get at me, not after what you did!

JOHN I was looking for the moment.

RICHARD Well you certainly got one!

JOHN Too much anger... we need something more... relatable.

RICHARD I swear to Christ!

HANNAH Thanks for throwing us under the bus.

RICHARD You let that bastard in.

HANNAH You told me to get someone.

RICHARD You didn't vet him!

HANNAH There was no time!

RICHARD And you let John run AMOK!

JOHN I did an Iraq!

HANNAH Because you were constantly undermining me.

RICHARD Ah for fuck sake. Take some responsibility!

HANNAH Then fucking give me some.

RICHARD You were making me look bad. It's my name on the credits!

JOHN The ratings'll be through the roof.

RICHARD I see it now. I go off to bury my wife, and everyone's plotting against me.

HANNAH What?

RICHARD You've figured out how to take me down, is it?

HANNAH Rich, calm down.

RICHARD The PM wants my head on a spike!

HANNAH You're stressed.

RICHARD She's right. We can't risk anything more. John you're asking the questions now. No more from the audience.

HANNAH We can't give up editorial control.

RICHARD Grow the fuck up Hannah.

HANNAH We hold them to account!

RICHARD We do what we're told.

JOHN I can handle it. I'll bring it back round.

RICHARD You better. You got us into this mess!

JOHN Ah, fuck off.

RICHARD Jumped up celebrity!

JOHN More integrity than you.

RICHARD Ha! Integrity! I could get Martha in here, she'd do a better job than you.

JOHN Don't you DARE talk about her!

HANNAH Rich!

JOHN Why weren't you on the line Rich?

RICHARD What?

JOHN If you weren't giving me permission to let him speak, what were you doing?

RICHARD I was... I was...

JOHN and HANNAH RICH!

RICH *suddenly cried out in anguish. Awkward pause.*

JOHN Rich?

RICHARD I shouldn't have... It was Grainne.

HANNAH What about her?

RICHARD She's, fuck. She's not doing well.

JOHN Her episodes?

RICHARD Yeah. *(Beat)* Says she's... she says she's seeing Niamh...

JOHN What? She thinks Niamh's still alive?

RICHARD No. She knows her mum's dead. But thinks she can see 'alternate realities', where Niamh hasn't died.

JOHN Christ.

RICHARD She's been like this for years! Once she said she saw a world in which Ireland was already independent, but part of the north's still in the UK.[81]

JOHN If anywhere would stay in the UK, it'd be Cork[82] – it's as British as Finchley.[83]

RICHARD She was always drawing this made up Irish flag, but it was just a bad Italian flag. And she used to go on about her brother.

JOHN You've a son?

RICHARD No, I don't know where she got that.

HANNAH Are you going to take her home?

---

[81] The partition of Ireland under the Government of Ireland Act 1920 divided the island of Ireland into two jurisdictions, Northern Ireland and Southern Ireland. Today, the former is still known as Northern Ireland and forms part of the United Kingdom, while the latter is now a sovereign state also named Ireland, Éire and sometimes called the Republic of Ireland.
[82] Cork is known as the 'Rebel county'. This nickname is often thought to have originated in its role in the Irish War of Independence, but it was given to the county by King Henry VII of England for its support of a man claiming to be Richard, Duke of York in a futile attempt at a rebellion.
[83] During The Troubles, British Prime Minister Margaret Thatcher made the claim that Northern Ireland was 'as British as Finchley'.

RICHARD She just drew a bad Italian flag.[84]

HANNAH Are you going to take her home?

RICHARD No.

HANNAH She can't be here.

JOHN How long have we got?

HANNAH Two minutes.

JOHN Sort it out.

    JOHN *walks back to his filming spot.*

RICHARD OK, this is what's happening. You take Grainne down to the canteen, get her some water –

HANNAH No.

RICHARD – and sit with her.

HANNAH I'm in the gallery tonight Rich. You're not taking that away from me.

RICHARD Do your job.

HANNAH I'm fuckin trying to!

RICHARD Your job is what I say it is.

HANNAH Rich, she's your daughter.

RICHARD Take her to the canteen.

HANNAH She's off her meds!

    Beat.

---

[84] The Irish flag, a vertical tri-colour of green, white and orange is similar to the Italian flag, a vertical tri-colour of green, white and red. The Irish flag was presented as a gift in 1848 to Irish nationalist Thomas Francis Meagher from a small group of French women sympathetic to the Irish cause. It was intended to symbolise the hoped-for union between Roman Catholics (green) and Protestants (orange). It was not until the Easter Rising of 1916 that the tricolour came to be regarded as the national flag of Ireland.

RICHARD No, she's not.

HANNAH She hasn't been taking them.

RICHARD I saw her take them.

    HANNAH *produces the packet of pills from her pocket.*

HANNAH She didn't swallow them. She threw them in the bin.

    Pause. HANNAH *gives the packet to* RICHARD.

Go to her. Take her home.

RICHARD No I have to be...

HANNAH I'm not saying this as her friend. I'm saying this as a producer.

RICHARD Assistant producer.

JOHN Hannah! How long?!

HANNAH About a minute!

JOHN Alright guys. Let's fucking go! Hannah, get the PM and Keogh back in here!

RICHARD You knew?

HANNAH What?

RICHARD You knew she was off her meds?

HANNAH Rich, we have to go!

RICHARD And you didn't tell me?

HANNAH She didn't want me to. I didn't want to get in the middle...

RICHARD You didn't want to get in the middle?! How fucking dare you!

HANNAH Rich, we've thirty seconds!

RICHARD She's not safe around herself and you left her. Jesus. I left her.

JOHN Rich, how do you want to do this?

RICHARD Fuck. Right. OK. *(Quickly)* Give them both a short statement. Get it over with quickly and move on. I have to go to Grainne. And you're asking the questions John, not the audience. Am I clear?

JOHN Crystal.

HANNAH Fifteen seconds!

RICHARD I'll deal with *you* later.

JOHN Right! Once more into the breach, dear friends. Let's set Ireland free. Let's save the Union. Whatever! Let's give them a good, balanced, impartial, sexy debate.

HANNAH Five, four, three ...Cue John!

Scene Three

Debate graphics and Intro music. Studio and gallery.

JOHN Fáilte ar ais chuig 'Ireland Decides'.[85] We apologise for the interruption. We at the BBC respect free speech, but we need to ensure that many opinions are heard tonight. We're now going to have a brief statement from each candidate before jumping straight back into questions. Prime Minister.

PM LYSAGHT Absolutely. Of course, this country is built on free speech. It's one of our dearest values. But we should respect everyone, and never discriminate on grounds of race, class or creed. Mr Keogh and I are going to finish the debate, presenting the arguments clearly and rationally, so you can make an informed choice.

KEOGH *(rolling up his sleeves and stepping out from the podium).* Thank you Ursula. This is what happens when people are left behind – they turn to the extremes. I absolutely do not condone what he said, but I understand his frustration. I am also very frustrated. So let me speak directly to him. *(Looking into the camera)* Young man, we want an Ireland for everyone. Instead of throwing blame at the blameless, you have a clear course of action. Use your vote. If you are dissatisfied with this government's lack of care, it's inability to represent you, show them tomorrow.

JOHN Thank you both. To avoid any more confusion, we won't be going to the audience. I will ask the questions for the remainder of the debate.

HANNAH VOICE OVER Defence.

JOHN Our first question is about Defence. 'Many people in Ireland are proud of their service. What will happen to the Irish regiments in the British Army?' Prime Minister?

---

[85] 'Welcome back to Ireland Decides'.

PM LYSAGHT Another thing the Leave campaign has no answer for. The only way to ensure our safety is to Remain. Irish people are proud of their service in the Army. Together we beat Hitler. Keogh comes from a tradition of Irish Nationalists who actually fought *for* the Nazis.

KEOGH Who are you referring to?

PM LYSAGHT One of Hitler's inner circle – Eddy De Valera.[86]

KEOGH Nonsense! De Valera wasn't Irish, he was American.

PM LYSAGHT He was Irish! He just used his American citizenship to get off at Nuremberg![87]

JOHN Eddy DeValera has no bearing on the question of Irish independence. We're talking about Defence.

PM LYSAGHT Certainly John. I ask Peter, how could we separate? What would happen to the Royal Navy base in Carlingford Lough?[88] Or RAF Galway? Could Ireland afford its own Navy and Airforce? I'd say we'd still be reliant on our English / neighbours to patrol our skies.[89]

---

[86] Eamon De Valera was a prominent political leader in 20th century Ireland. From 1917 to 1973; he served several terms as head of government and head of state. He also led the introduction of the Constitution of Ireland. Under his government, Ireland was neutral in WW2, and was accused of Nazi sympathy by the British and Northern Irish governments. Upon the death of Adolf Hitler, De Valera controversially offered his condolences to the German Minister in Dublin. As a child, he was known as 'Eddy'.

[87] Prior to De Valera's political career, he was a Commandant at Boland's Mill during the 1916 Easter Rising, an Irish revolution that eventually led to Irish independence. He was arrested, sentenced to death but released due to public response to the British executions of the Rising leaders, and because he had American citizenship.

[88] Carlingford Lough is a glacial fjord or sea inlet that forms part of the border between Northern Ireland to the north and the Republic of Ireland to the south. Similarly as with Lough Foyle, a body of water between Donegal and Derry, the exact position of the border in Carlingford Lough is still disputed between the British and Irish governments.

[89] In 2016, the Irish press reported that Irish government had entered into a bilateral agreement with the British government permitting the British military to conduct armed operations inside Irish airspace in the event of a real-time or envisaged threat of an aerial terrorist-related attack on Ireland or on a neighbouring country.

KEOGH This is a common tactic from Ms Lysaght.

PM LYSAGHT Can I finish?

KEOGH She'll bring up dozens of questions to / dazzle and...

PM LYSAGHT Questions which need / answers.

KEOGH ...dazzle and shock and scare you!

PM LYSAGHT What scares me is your lack of a plan, Mr Keogh.

HANNAH VOICE OVER Get a hold of them John.

JOHN Do you have a plan Mr Keogh?

KEOGH My party holds up your government, Prime Minister. *(To audience)* She doesn't care about the Irish people or this referendum. She only cares about her own skin.

PM LYSAGHT And Mr Keogh only deals in threats.

KEOGH The Prime Minister would never have given you a say on your future, if she wasn't desperately holding onto power!

JOHN Mr Keogh, please.

KEOGH Without Irish MPs in Westminster propping up Labour governments, there'd be permanent Tory rule in Britain. That's what scares the Prime Minister – losing her own job!

JOHN The question is about the Army.

KEOGH The fact is: I don't have the answers to her questions. But the Irish people do. In an Iindependent Ireland these questions will all be answered. By referenda, by parliamentary votes, by citizens, committees. So don't worry about the uncertainty. Embrace the possibilities. And notice, the last great thing she mentioned the British Army did was beating Hitler. I think the Irish public are more concerned with more recent actions: the illegal war in Iraq, the thousands dead in Afghanistan. This is what people think of when they think of the British Army. The Irish people want peace, not war.[90]

Lights snap down on studio and gallery (including video), and lights up on office.

RICHARD *walks into the office. He stands for a moment.* **GRAINNE** *sits.*

GRAINNE Are you alright?

RICHARD I've been better.

GRAINNE The debate's back on?

GRAINNE They're already at each other's throats.

GRAINNE Who was he?

RICHARD Some lunatic. The famine? By Christ, who even remembers the famine?

GRAINNE The Genocide you mean.

RICHARD Nationalist propaganda. It's not the Prime Minister's fault our ancestors were too thick to grow carrots as well as spuds.

GRAINNE Well, that's just government propaganda.

RICHARD He went off on a racist tandem.

Beat. **GRAINNE** *is embarrassed at the dad joke.*

GRAINNE Tangent.

RICHARD A racist tandem bicycle. Him on the front, a KKK fella on the back.

GRAINNE *doesn't laugh.*

---

[90] Ireland has been neutral in international relations since the 1930s. Historically, the state was a 'non-belligerent' in the Second World War and has never joined NATO. The compatibility of neutrality with Ireland's membership of the European Union has been a point of debate in EU treaty referendum campaigns since the 1990s.

GRAINNE How did he get in?

RICHARD He was sitting in your seat.

GRAINNE I suppose it's my fault then?

RICHARD No. It was Hannah's. I know she's your friend Grainne, but Jesus.

GRAINNE You spend a lot of time with Hannah.

RICHARD And this is how she repays me.

GRAINNE You gave her the show to run.

RICHARD I did. So I could be here with you. Why didn't you take your—

GRAINNE 'She goes or I go'.

RICHARD What do you mean?

GRAINNE Makes sense why she wasn't at the funeral.

RICHARD What are you on about?

GRAINNE Why she wouldn't help me find out the truth. Why it wasn't her place.

RICHARD Grainne, listen to me / I'm trying to –

GRAINNE How predictable can you be! Sleeping with your assistant.

RICHARD What? Sleeping with Hannah!?

GRAINNE When did Mum find out?

RICHARD What are you talking about?

GRAINNE How long has it been going on for? Was it when we were still in school?

RICHARD Don't be ridiculous.

GRAINNE Why's it ridiculous? You spend a lot of time together.

RICHARD Well, yes. I work with her.

GRAINNE So you never did?

RICHARD No!

GRAINNE Never thought about it?

RICHARD I would never think of cheating on your mother.

GRAINNE That night Mum was getting away from something –
from you.

RICHARD No.

GRAINNE You slept with Hannah. Mum found out. That's why
she left.

RICHARD I never slept with Hannah!

GRAINNE That's why Hannah wasn't at the funeral.

RICHARD She was working!

GRAINNE She was ashamed! And in my break I'm seeing a
world where mum never found out the truth.

RICHARD Your breaks!

GRAINNE So she didn't leave. So she didn't crash the car. That's it.

RICHARD In any of them. In the millions of your alternate
worlds. Did I cheat on your mum in any of them?

GRAINNE No.

RICHARD Because I couldn't. Trust me.

GRAINNE But what about in this reality Dad?

RICHARD Please stop this. Take your medication.

GRAINNE How do you know I'm not?

RICHARD *produces the packet of* GRAINNE's *pills he got
from* HANNAH.

Beat.

She told you.

RICHARD What is this Grainne, a cry for help?

GRAINNE Fuck that.

RICHARD I won't see you go through this again.

GRAINNE I'm not taking them.

RICHARD If you need stronger stuff, we'll get you to the doctor.

GRAINNE No. I want the breaks. I don't care if it hurts me.

RICHARD She's gone. Accept it.

GRAINNE That's what everyone's told me my whole life. 'Just accept it'. Can you imagine what it's like when you're told to accept things that you know aren't true?

RICHARD That's why we got you help.

GRAINNE I gave in.

RICHARD Please take them, I'm scared / of what will happen...

GRAINNE I'm scared too. I'm fuckin terrified of stopping taking them. I'm not fucking enjoying this! But when I don't take them, I can see Mum! And I don't want that to stop. Dad why won't you talk to me about what happened?

RICHARD It's not the time.

GRAINNE When is the fucking time, Dad?

RICHARD Take your medication. I just want you to be safe.

GRAINNE I am safe. Why are you lying to me about Mum?

RICHARD I'm not lying.

GRAINNE Then why are you being so fucking weird?!

RICHARD Take your medication.

GRAINNE Fuck. You.

> GRAINNE *moves to leave.* RICHARD *runs over and blocks the door.*

RICHARD Where are you going?

GRAINNE Home.

RICHARD Wait until the debate's over! We'll go /together.

GRAINNE Fucking hell. You and that debate!

RICHARD We've had enough disruption tonight.

GRAINNE Is all you think about your fucking job?

RICHARD It's the referendum!

GRAINNE Who the fuck cares about the referendum? It won't change anything!

RICHARD This from the girl who doesn't want to talk politics.

Lights go up on the studio and gallery and the two scenes now take place at the exact same time.

JOHN Another question:

RICHARD Take them.

JOHN 'If Leave wins, what will Keogh do to protect British culture and identity?'[91]

GRAINNE No.

JOHN Maybe we should go to Peter first?

GRAINNE I want to see her again.

PM LYSAGHT Absolutely.

RICHARD *takes two pills out of the packet and holds them out.*

RICHARD Blame me all you want, but take them.

KEOGH I, in no way, want to diminish the rights...

GRAINNE I won't.

KEOGH ...or the culture of the British people on this island.

RICHARD Grainne, don't defy me.

---

[91] A question often posed to the supporters of Irish Unification is how to protect the British culture that exists within Northern Ireland.

GRAINNE You don't control me.

KEOGH An independent Ireland is about self-determination.

RICHARD Just take them.

GRAINNE No.

KEOGH It's about the rights of the people of this island to choose the future of this island.

RICHARD *points the pills at* **GRAINNE**. *She shakes her head.*

RICHARD Fucking take them!

GRAINNE MUUUUUUM!

He grabs her hand and places a pill in it. She throws it down. He takes two more pills from the packet and places them in her other hand, she throws them in his face. He takes more pills from the packet. In a quick movement, **RICHARD** *moves behind* **GRAINNE** *and grabs her around the neck. He forcibly tries to push the pills into her mouth, pushing* **GRAINNE** *onto the desk, knocking the bust of Cromwell to the floor.* **GRAINNE** *struggles and rips the headset off* **RICHARD**.

KEOGH I envision an independent Ireland with close cultural and economic links with The United Kingdom. Not 'cutting ourselves off' from our closest neighbour, but forging our own path alongside them. In my mind an independent Ireland will still proudly have Orange marches[92] alongside Saint Patrick's Day parades.

---

[92] 'Orange marches' are a series of parades held annually by members of the Orange Order during the summer in Northern Ireland. These typically build up to 12 July celebrations, which mark Prince William of Orange's victory over King James II at the Battle of the Boyne in 1690. Orange marches have faced opposition from Irish nationalists who see the parades as sectarian and triumphalist.

GRAINNE *struggles with* RICHARD. *He nearly gets the pills in her mouth, but she closes it tight. Still holding her from behind,* RICHARD *pinches her nose closed.*

RICHARD Take. Your. Meds.

JOHN Prime Minister.

PM LYSAGHT This question gets to the heart of what this debate is about. Most people will vote tomorrow based on whether they feel more British or more Irish. I think that is dangerous. What we need, is to maintain a strong Irish identity within the UK. People should be comfortable to feel both British *and* Irish – they are not mutually exclusive. Keogh cannot deliver that, no matter how much he talks about inclusivity.

Eventually, GRAINNE *has to open her mouth to breathe and* RICHARD *forces the pills in – one hand over her mouth and the other forcibly massaging her throat to ensure she swallows. They stay locked together like this for an uncomfortably long time.*

KEOGH The United Kingdom can never accommodate the Irish identity!

PM LYSAGHT You can't force an exclusionary identity onto people who do not want it.

KEOGH We will not be placated by the scraps thrown to us by our British overlords.

HANNAH Thirty seconds to ad break.

PM LYSAGHT Britain IS Ireland. 'sé Éireann an Bhreatain![93] The only solution is a strong Ireland within the United Kingdom.

GRAINNE *slumps to the ground, almost passed out.* RICHARD *hurriedly steps over her, inspects her mouth to make sure the pills have gone.*

---

[93] 'Ireland is Britain'.

KEOGH Which is abhorrent to any self-respecting Irish person! Ní thuigfá.

PM LYSAGHT Don't you dare tell me I am not Irish! Níl leatsa atá an chinneadh faoin Éireannachas![94]

KEOGH Ní leatsa ach an oiread a Chailleach Bhriotánach![97.5]

JOHN We'll hold it there. Time for our final ad break. We'll be right back with the final segment of 'Ireland Decides'

RICHARD storms out of the door, shutting it behind him, locking her in. As he shuts it, lights snap down on the debate. **RICHARD** *leans against the door, taking a moment to himself.* **GRAINNE** *is alone the office, slumped and shivering. She twitches and open her eyes.*

GRAINNE Mum.

The lights flicker.

Mum! Mum, I'm here!

GRAINNE *puts her fingers down her throat. She tries to force out the pills. She retches. She retches again over the bin, but cannot vomit. She sits down and cries. The lights flicker seriously and the TV signal scrambles and the audio bellows, and we clearly see* **GRAINNE**'s *break – on the screen –* **NIAMH** *is in tears.*

Did he attack you? Is that why you left?

The lights blackout. As if a fuse has blown. The audio swell dissipates. The video image scrambles and begins to fall away. The 'break' fizzles out. **GRAINNE** *is in the dark.*

No! No! Mum! Come back!

---

[94] 'You don't get to decide what Irishness is!'
[97.5] 'And neither do you, you British witch'

Scene Four

News report.

REPORTER More drama at BBC Dublin, which has become the epicentre of chaos in the city tonight. After a young man was removed from the studio for threatening the Prime Minister, the marches in the streets became violent, with clashes between Leave supporters and police. Remainers also engaged in rioting as bricks and rocks were thrown, and reportedly shots were fired. The police retaliated by firing tear gas and plastic bullets.[95] There have been a number of injuries.

RICHARD *walks up to the edge of the gallery and gestures for* **HANNAH** *to come out. She is on headset and looking at her phone.*

HANNAH What is it Rich?

RICHARD When are we back on?

HANNAH Three minutes, after the report on the riots.

RICHARD Riots? When the fuck did that happen?!

HANNAH The marches. *(Reading off her phone)* Looks like stones were thrown. An RIC[96] officer hit someone. They're chanting 'BREHON LAW, NOT SHARIA LAW'.

HANNAH *goes to move back into the gallery.*

RICHARD This is your fault.

---

[95] Plastic bullets were invented in 1973 by the British security forces for use against rioters in Northern Ireland.

Shortly after their introduction it was discovered they were lethal at certain ranges. Fourteen people were killed by plastic bullet impacts; half of them were children and all but one were from the Catholic community.
[96] The Royal Irish Constabulary was the police force in Ireland from the early nineteenth century until independence in 1922, when they were replaced by An Garda Síochána, more commonly referred to as the Gardaí or 'the Guards'.

HANNAH Don't take this out on me.

RICHARD You fucked up!

HANNAH You should have stayed at home with Grainne.

RICHARD The strings I've pulled to fast track / you through this place...

HANNAH I need to get back to my job.

RICHARD ...to fast track you through the ranks...

HANNAH Sorry. It was *you* who told me to fill that seat with some randomer.

RICHARD ...and I'm surprised...

HANNAH It was *you* who wasn't there for John / when –

RICHARD John's a fuckstick. And you were the one in the gallery!

HANNAH And you were in his ear!

RICHARD Take the initiative!

HANNAH How can I when you're over my shoulder /second guessing everything I do?

RICHARD Well I'm not doing that anymore. You're just not cut out for this. I'm calling the show.

HANNAH No you're not.

RICHARD This is my studio. I'm the producer.

HANNAH I'm wrapping it up. You're in no state to run this.

RICHARD Give me that headset.

HANNAH Not when you're like this.

RICHARD Shut up and do what you're told or get the fuck out of my studio and never come back!

HANNAH Do as I'm told? Like you're doing what the PM told you?

RICHARD Don't be so naive Hannah.

HANNAH I'm finishing this debate.

HANNAH moves as if to go back into the gallery. RICHARD *violently grabs the headset off* HANNAH'*s head and wrestles the radio pack off her. It's a very violent act.*

What the fuck?

RICHARD First, I have to deal with Grainne. Now you. Am I the only one who can hold this shit together?

HANNAH What do you mean 'deal with Grainne'? What did you do?

RICHARD She's safe.

HANNAH moves to leave.

Where are you going?

HANNAH To Grainne.

RICHARD Don't fuckin go anywhere near her!

HANNAH Why?

RICHARD If you go up to her, you're never coming back.

Beat.

HANNAH Really?

Beat.

RICHARD I swear Hannah. You sit in here with me, or you're done.

HANNAH looks at RICHARD. *She turns and walks away.* RICHARD *looks like he might follow her, but he hears a noise on his headset.*

Shit! *(Into headset)* It's Rich. 10 seconds till we're live!

RICHARD *rushes into the gallery. Lights down on gallery and lights up on office.* HANNAH *runs up the stairs.* GRAINNE *sits against the door, barricading it.*

HANNAH *bangs on the door.*

HANNAH Grainne, it's—

GRAINNE Go away.

HANNAH *opens the door with her keycard. The office has been wrecked.*

HANNAH Fuck! Grainne, what happened?

Beat.

HANNAH What did he do?

GRAINNE I'm sorry, I thought it was because of you.

HANNAH What do you mean?

GRAINNE I thought you were sleeping together.

HANNAH Who? Me and your dad?

GRAINNE Yeah.

HANNAH What the fuck Grainne? He's ancient, no offense like but no.

GRAINNE I know. I was wrong. She was just trying to get away from him.

HANNAH What?

GRAINNE Jesus what did he do to her?

HANNAH Grainne, are you OK? Look at me.

Beat.

Tell me what happened here.

GRAINNE He made me take my pills.

HANNAH Right, well. You should be taking them.

GRAINNE He forced me.

HANNAH Like, physically?

GRAINNE *nods.*

Fuck.

GRAINNE I shut my mouth, but he grabbed my nose and—

HANNAH Jesus.

GRAINNE I struggled. I tried. I did, I tried. But I couldn't breathe. I had to open my mouth. And he forced them down my throat.

Beat.

HANNAH That's assault Grainne. Fuck me... I knew he was... but fucking hell.

GRAINNE You knew he was what?

HANNAH I knew he was ruthless. I've seen him turn before. But this is / something else.

GRAINNE He's not the same. Since Mum died.

HANNAH No, he's just fired me...

GRAINNE He fired you?

HANNAH ...and grabbed my headset, and he's abusing you. He's dangerous.

GRAINNE What did he do to Mum that night? What the fuck is going on Hannah?!

HANNAH The shit I've put up with over the years, because Rich said that's how it worked. But it's all fucked isn't it?

GRAINNE Yeah.

HANNAH He'd get out of it. Let's just go. We'll have time / to come up with a plan.

GRAINNE No we have to do it now! Before the vote. If we don't get him now, he'll get his fuckin MBE and he'll be shaking hands with the Queen. We'll confront him. Me and you.

HANNAH No, he'll do something. You know what he's like.

GRAINNE We'll phone the police.

HANNAH A skitzo and a fired producer? They won't believe us.

GRAINNE We'll explain...

HANNAH They'll lie. Rich is so far up the PM's hole.

GRAINNE We need to do something.

HANNAH *What* then?

GRAINNE I don't know! I need the truth. I came here for that. It's a fuckin newsroom you think you'd be able to get some fuckin truth.

HANNAH Not in this newsroom.

GRAINNE I'm not leaving until I find out what happened to my mum. Help me Hannah!

HANNAH I'm sorry, Grainne.

GRAINNE I need to get him to listen.

HANNAH I'm sorry. I haven't been there for you.

GRAINNE We need to pin him down.

HANNAH I was so fuckin worried about pleasing him, about keeping my job, working my way up. And he's throwing me under a bus, firing me, fuckin' assaulting you. He should be fired, not me.

GRAINNE We need to corner him.

HANNAH The whole system's fucked.

GRAINNE At least the rioters are doing something.

HANNAH It won't make any difference. They'll just show clips of it in the news, label them all racists and ignore them.

GRAINNE Of course they ignore them! They're outside the system.

HANNAH Well, it needs to change.

GRAINNE How?

HANNAH I dunno. Fuck, I know he was a racist but at least your man earlier got people's attention.

GRAINNE Everyone listened to *him*.

HANNAH He wasn't ignored.

GRAINNE In front of all the cameras.

HANNAH He changed the conversation.

GRAINNE In front of the whole country.

Beat. They look at each other. They see **RICHARD**'s *headset on the desk.*

They look at it. They look back to each other.

HANNAH Grainne...

GRAINNE Hannah.

HANNAH I can't.

GRAINNE I have to do this.

HANNAH You're not well. I can't let you.

GRAINNE He has to know that he can't silence me.

Scene Five

Studio and gallery. RICHARD *is in the gallery on* HANNAH's *headset.*

PM LYSAGHT ...which is why you should be worried about healthcare in an independent Ireland.

RICHARD *(on earpiece)* Wrap this up John. Closing arguments and we can get out of here.

KEOGH I'd like to ask Ursula how she feels about the riots tearing through Dublin?

RICHARD Fuck, shut it down John.

JOHN Riots Prime Minister? What do you say to that.

PM LYSAGHT Peter Keogh will do anything to get out of talking about healthcare, but all right. The people in the streets are fueled by hatred. This Leave campaign, with Peter Keogh at its helm, it preaches hate. Hatred of foreigners. Hatred of fellow Britons. Hatred, is not something I think of when I think of the Irish people. Friendliness, inclusion, agus fonn oibriú le chéile.[97]

RICHARD You've had your fun, now wrap it up.

JOHN Hatred? First Minister Keogh, your response?

KEOGH Thank you John. We've heard a lot from Prime Minister Lysaght today. A lot of fear. Fear of loss of jobs, a lack of future, fear of what the Irish people are capable of. That fear is dangerous. I appeal for calm, and tell those rioters, they need not be afraid. Tomorrow they will make a democratic choice for the betterment of this nation, and it should be inspired by hope. Not driven by fear.

RICHARD *(in earpiece)* Move it on.

PM LYSAGHT You're fueling the fear!

---

[97] 'a willingness to work together'.

JOHN Thank you. Now we're going –

KEOGH Are you calling my supporters racists again Mrs Lysaght?!

JOHN We've been over this Mr Keogh.

PM LYSAGHT Now when I said that I certainly didn't mean to imply –

RICHARD *(in earpiece)* John.

KEOGH The people are in the streets, and your Prime Minister is calling you racist! For making a democratic choice.

JOHN Mr Keogh!

KEOGH That is not how you keep the peace!

RICHARD *(in earpiece)* John, stabilise this / now.

PM LYSAGHT It's you that's breaking the peace!

JOHN Are you accusing Mr Keogh of inciting riots?

RICHARD *(in earpiece)* Fuck sake John, you're a disgrace.

 JOHN *looks directly into the camera.*

PM LYSAGHT If the cap fits Mr Keogh, if the cap fits.

RICHARD Stop fucking around, we're out of time!

JOHN Very very interesting.

RICHARD *(in earpiece)* You're a washed up has-been. You fucked it. Who'd hire you after tonight?

 HANNAH *is in the office, wearing* **RICHARD**'s *headset. Awkward pause on the studio floor as* **JOHN** *listens to the following dialogue.*

HANNAH John, we actually have time for one more question. Say that.

RICHARD Hannah? What are you doing?

HANNAH You want that job at SKY, John?

RICHARD Don't you dare.

HANNAH This is your moment.

RICHARD I'll get Martha to strangle you with that fucking tie!

Beat. **JOHN** *straightens his tie.*

JOHN I'm actually just hearing we have time for one more question.

HANNAH It's coming from...

JOHN *(repeating as* **HANNAH** *says it)* It's coming from...

HANNAH Grainne.

RICHARD Grainne?

JOHN It's coming from Grainne?

> **GRAINNE** *walks down the middle of the audience, holding a microphone.*

GRAINNE Ummm...hello, yes. I have a question.

RICHARD What is this?

PM LYSAGHT *(under her breath)* John, no questions from the floor.

RICHARD John, you piece of shit! Don't take it.

> **JOHN** *removes his earpiece so he can no longer hear* **RICHARD** *or* **HANNAH**.

JOHN Yes Grainne. What's your question?

RICHARD John, cut her off!

HANNAH He can't hear you anymore.

> **RICHARD** *throws off his headset and runs out of the gallery into the studio in panic. He stands at the edge of the floor, panicked.*

GRAINNE Yeah, I'd like to...sorry there's a lot of people.

JOHN It's OK Grainne. We've heard a lot from the politicians tonight. I think it's good we end on a question from someone who this vote will actually affect. Take your time. Can we have a camera on Grainne, please?

PM LYSAGHT I'm not sure the young lady wants a camera on her...

KEOGH Let's take your question young lady. We'll answer as best we can. We all want what's best for the country.

GRAINNE The *country*? The *country*. You all talk about what's best for *the country*. But none of you care about the *people*. You keep us in the dark.

PM LYSAGHT Grainne was it? We care deeply about the people.

JOHN Grainne, I know it's hard. These are uncertain times. Do you have a question for the Leave or Remain campaigns?

GRAINNE Leave, Remain, Leave, Remain, who gives a fuck?!

JOHN The passion's great Grainne, but let's keep it civil.

GRAINNE It doesn't matter. I've seen independent Irelands where the people are broken, chained to a pulpit, and I've seen them where no-one goes hungry and everyone has a home.

JOHN What do you mean you've 'seen'?

GRAINNE I've seen Ireland's within Britain flourish and I've seen the Irish beaten down and subjugated by governments in London *and* in Dublin. British, Irish, whatever. It doesn't matter who our rulers are – it matters how much we demand to be listened to.

JOHN Well you're certainly demanding to be listened to now. Let's have your question.

GRAINNE My question is for Richard.

JOHN For...

GRAINNE For my dad. Richard.

HANNAH Get a camera on him.

RICHARD Grainne?

GRAINNE The producer of this show.

RICHARD Grainne why are you doing this?

GRAINNE I want to ask him why he force-fed me medication...

JOHN He did what?

HANNAH Keep it live!

RICHARD Grainne, sit down!

GRAINNE ...why he pinned me down, put a hand over my mouth and forced me to take medication I didn't want. I want to know why...

JOHN How could a father do such a thing?

RICHARD She's sick!

PM LYSAGHT What's this?

KEOGH Mad stuff John.

GRAINNE ...I want to know why he drove my mother out of the house?

JOHN We're so sorry to hear that Grainne.

HANNAH Keep it going.

RICHARD GRAINNE! Stop this now!

HANNAH Keep it going!

GRAINNE Letting her to drive through the pouring rain...

RICHARD She's not stable.

JOHN Absolutely heart-breaking.

GRAINNE Until she crashed her car...

RICHARD She's delusional.

GRAINNE ... the steering wheel through her chest...

RICHARD STOP IT!

GRAINNE ...bleeding to death in a ditch...

RICHARD Grainne, PLEASE!

GRAINNE ...as he sat at home...

RICHARD She left us!

GRAINNE ...smiling to himself...

RICHARD She was trying to get away from YOU! She abandoned YOU!

Silence. GRAINNE *stands for a moment, speechless. After a moment, she drops the microphone and walks out.* RICHARD *stands in shock.*

HANNAH Cut. Cut to advert!

The lights dim. On the screens we see the Debate graphics fade to black. The transmission light goes off.

PM LYSAGHT I'm done. This is a fuckin shambles. *(She pulls out her phone and starts talking into it as she walks off stage)* Put out a statement, mental health, NHS, provisions for that type of thing, can't be protected in an independent Ireland, sorry for what she's going through, all that shite.

PM LYSAGHT *walks offstage.*

KEOGH Thanks for that Rich. You certainly know how to do interesting TV. Never a dull moment.

KEOGH *walks offstage in the opposite direction.*

RICHARD *slowly turns and walks to* JOHN.

RICHARD You.

JOHN I thought I handled it very well.

RICHARD You let my disturbed daughter / stand up in front of...

JOHN I just let her talk. You attacked her.

RICHARD I helped her.

HANNAH *(into her headset)* The politicians are out.

RICHARD It was for her own good—

HANNAH *(into her headset)* Let's go back to John to wrap up.

JOHN I was trying to be compassionate.

RICHARD You were using her!

JOHN I was doing my job! It was a good moment.

RICHARD Yeah, you and your fuckin moment. You're out of control.

JOHN You've lost it Rich!

RICHARD Selfish bastard!

JOHN Go home and grieve!

RICHARD You glory-seeking shit stain!

JOHN Shit stain?!

HANNAH *(into her headset)* Back in ten seconds.

JOHN The way you treat her – you might as well keep her on a leash!

RICHARD I'll make sure no-one hires you!

JOHN What kind of father are you?

HANNAH *(into her headset)* five, four, three...

RICHARD A Booterstown asshole with delusions of grandeur! You've no principles!

JOHN *and* RICHARD *appear on screen again. The transmission light is on.*

They are live.

JOHN And you do? You drugged your own daughter!

RICHARD To keep her safe! You wouldn't understand. You only care about yourself! You don't even give a damn about this island.

JOHN Would you stop with this romanticism! Ireland this! Ireland that! It's a shit-hole. Full of shit-eating, inbred bog people who begrudge anyone with a bit of success.

JOHN *looks into the camera. He realises they have been speaking live on air.*

JOHN Um... Welcome back. Clearly emotions are running very high.

HANNAH There's your fucking moment, John.

Scene Six

News report.

...these riots moved towards BBC Dublin, where leaders of both campaigns were participating in the 'Ireland Decides' debate. The Prime Minister and Irish First Minister have both called for calm, but it was the second interruption of the debate, this time by a young woman, that caused the Prime Minister to walk out. Reports are that the young woman was related to the producer of the programme and accused him of assault. It is thought the referendum vote will still go ahead tomorrow, but there is much anger in the capital, and uncertainty over which way the people will vote.

Scene Seven

An empty studio, except for **RICHARD** *who is sitting on the floor with his head in his hands. The pace is much slower, the dialogue more gentle, with greater use of silence.*

GRAINNE *enters. She walks over to* **RICHARD,** *but does not sit next to him.*

GRAINNE Where's everyone?

RICHARD *(shocked)* The Prime Minister and Keogh have been smuggled out. The audience is holed up in the canteen. Waiting for the riots to subside.

Beat.

John's probably crying somewhere after losing his chance of a London job. So, you know, every cloud.

GRAINNE Sorry I ruined your debate.

RICHARD We'll blame it on John. He can be our 'escaped goat'.

GRAINNE *doesn't laugh. Long pause.*

GRAINNE 'She goes or I go'. She meant me, didn't she?

Beat. **RICHARD** *nods.*

You were arguing about me.

RICHARD We were always arguing, love.

GRAINNE But that night was worse. Why?

RICHARD Because of this bloody referendum.

GRAINNE What?

Silence. **RICHARD** *looks at* **GRAINNE.**

RICHARD We were fighting about how we'd vote... the uncertainty of everything, what if we couldn't get your medication? But

she wanted things to change. And then we got into a big
disagreement over your future.

GRAINNE What about it?

RICHARD She wanted you to live on your own after your degree.
Go off and live your own life. I thought you needed to stay
with us. But she thought it would be the best thing for you.
And also for her.

GRAINNE She goes or I go.

RICHARD She had to do everything. Make sure you took your
medication, get you out of bed in the morning... I was barely
there to help at the best of times, and the last few weeks...
I was constantly at work covering the referendum. I was
never at home. She just, she couldn't cope.

GRAINNE So she abandoned me.

RICHARD We had a row that night, and when you had an episode,
she said, 'You know what, if you want her to stay so badly,
you try it. You look after her'.

GRAINNE She drove off, when I was having a break.

RICHARD She would have come back Grainne. I've no doubt
about that. She would have come back if it wasn't for the
accident. Grainne, she loved you so much. Never think
anything else.

GRAINNE Where was she going?

RICHARD I dunno.

GRAINNE I killed her.

RICHARD No you didn't Grainne.

GRAINNE She left because of me.

RICHARD No Grainne.

GRAINNE I killed her.

RICHARD I knew you'd blame yourself. You can't think like that. It's not one thing. What if she'd taken a different road? What if it hadn't been raining? What if I'd stopped her? I nearly did. I nearly forced the keys out of her hand. If only I'd done that. Don't blame yourself Grainne, we argued over you, but we both wanted what was best for you.

GRAINNE Dad, you keep saying...

RICHARD We both loved you so much.

GRAINNE Dad! Listen to me.

Long pause.

You keep saying you and Mum both wanted 'what's best for me'. Did you ever think of asking me? I was there the whole time. If I'm to live in this world, I need to understand it. And then I can decide what I want to do. Yeah if I left, I'd probably fuck it up, have regrets, but so fuckin what? Probably fuck it up anyway if I stayed. Let me fail. Let me do that so I can learn and grow like a normal human being.

RICHARD I didn't want you to get hurt.

GRAINNE Dad, I'd rather make my own decisions and get it wrong than have them made for me. You could only see one possibility. But there's fuckin millions Dad. If you stopped trying to control everything, maybe you could see them.

RICHARD I didn't want you to get hurt.

GRAINNE You force-fed me pills.

Long pause. **HANNAH** *enters.*

HANNAH They say the riot has dispersed. We should be able to go now.

GRAINNE *walks towards* **HANNAH. RICHARD** *calls after her.*

RICHARD Your mother had a stillbirth.

GRAINNE *stops.*

A boy. He died in the womb... Your twin.

GRAINNE William.

RICHARD We never understood where you heard that.

Beat. GRAINNE *goes to leave again.*

How did she look? Your mother?

GRAINNE What?

RICHARD You saw her? In...

GRAINNE Yes.

RICHARD How is she?

GRAINNE She's...

RICHARD Did she say anything? How is she?

GRAINNE She's dead, Dad.

Beat.

GRAINNE *looks at* RICHARD *and walks towards* HANNAH. *She looks back at him, and then leaves with* HANNAH, *without a goodbye.*

RICHARD *is left there on his own. After a moment,* JOHN *enters, his tie loosened around his neck. He carries a bottle of Bushmills and two glasses. He sits beside* RICHARD. *He pours two drams of whiskey and waits in silence. After a moment...*

JOHN I think you owe me an apology.

RICHARD I'm sorry, John. *(Beat)* I'm sorry you're such a wanker.

They drink.

She's gone, John.

JOHN I know.

RICHARD I assume SKY haven't been in touch?

JOHN *gives* RICHARD *a look and knocks back a whiskey.*

Sorry for your loss.

JOHN You can't win them all.

Beat. They drink.

How do you think the vote will go now?

RICHARD I dunno. Leave or Remain...will it make a difference?

JOHN You've changed your tune.

RICHARD *shrugs. Beat.* JOHN *pours each of them another whiskey.*

RICHARD What a fuckin circus. Couldn't have ballsed it up more.

RICHARD *drinks his whiskey.*

JOHN I thought I handled it very well.

Blackout.

VISIT THE SAMUEL FRENCH BOOKSHOP AT THE ROYAL COURT THEATRE

Browse plays and theatre books, get expert advice and enjoy a coffee

Samuel French Bookshop
Royal Court Theatre
Sloane Square
London
SW1W 8AS
020 7565 5024

Shop from thousands of titles on our website

 samuelfrench.co.uk

 samuelfrenchltd

 samuel french uk

JOHN *gives* **RICHARD** *a look and knocks back a whiskey.*

Sorry for your loss.

JOHN You can't win them all.

Beat. They drink.

How do you think the vote will go now?

RICHARD I dunno. Leave or Remain...will it make a difference?

JOHN You've changed your tune.

RICHARD *shrugs. Beat.* **JOHN** *pours each of them another whiskey.*

RICHARD What a fuckin circus. Couldn't have ballsed it up more.

RICHARD *drinks his whiskey.*

JOHN I thought I handled it very well.

Blackout.

VISIT THE SAMUEL FRENCH BOOKSHOP AT THE ROYAL COURT THEATRE

Browse plays and theatre books, get expert advice and enjoy a coffee

Samuel French Bookshop
Royal Court Theatre
Sloane Square
London
SW1W 8AS
020 7565 5024

Shop from thousands of titles on our website

 samuelfrench.co.uk

 samuelfrenchltd

 samuel french uk